RUDOLF STEINER (1861–1925) called his spiritual philosophy 'anthroposophy', meaning 'wisdom of the human being'. As a highly developed seer, he based his work on direct knowledge and perception of spiritual dimensions. He initiated a modern and universal 'science of spirit', accessible to anyone willing to exercise clear and unprejudiced thinking.

From his spiritual investigations Steiner provided suggestions for the renewal of many activities, including education (both general and special), agriculture, medicine, economics, architecture, science, philosophy, religion and the arts. Today there are thousands of schools, clinics, farms and other organizations involved in practical work based on his principles. His many published works feature his research into the spiritual nature of the human being, the evolution of the world and humanity, and methods of personal development. Steiner wrote some 30 books and delivered over 6000 lectures across Europe. In 1924 he founded the General Anthroposophical Society, which today has branches throughout the world.

MINDFULNESS AND REVERENCE

Steps in Perception

RUDOLF STEINER

Selected and compiled by Andreas Neider

RUDOLF STEINER PRESS

Translated by Johanna Collis

Rudolf Steiner Press,
Hillside House, The Square
Forest Row, RH18 5ES

www.rudolfsteinerpress.com

Published by Rudolf Steiner Press 2017

Originally published in German under the title *Andacht und Achtsamkeit, Stufen des Wahrnehmens* by Futurum Verlag, Basel, in 2014

© Futurum Verlag 2014
This translation © Rudolf Steiner Press 2017

All quotations from Rudolf Steiner's *Knowledge of the Higher Worlds* are taken from the translation by D.S. Osmond and C. Davy, Rudolf Steiner Press 2011

A catalogue record for this book is available from the British Library

Print book ISBN: 978 1 85584 536 7
Ebook ISBN: 978 1 85584 496 4

Cover by Morgan Creative
Typeset by DP Photosetting, Neath, West Glamorgan
Printed and bound by 4Edge Ltd., Essex

Contents

Introduction

The Four Maxims of the Wisdom of the Pillars

J

In pure thought you find
The self that can support itself.

If you transform thought into image
You experience creating wisdom.

B

If you condense feeling into light
You reveal the formative force.

Objectify the will into being
And you create in world-being.

In the sense of these 'four maxims of the wisdom of the pillars',[1] the anthroposophical path of schooling and meditation rests upon two pillars exemplifying the two trees which according to legend abide in paradise: the Tree of Knowledge (J or Jakim) and the Tree of Life (B or Boas). In view of the challenges facing us in today's civilization it does seem imperative that we should pay attention not only to the Tree of Knowledge but also, even more urgently, to the Tree of Life. The exercises, meditations and further indications given by Rudolf Steiner and quoted in this book are here intended as aids in this quest.

Many readers who are familiar with anthroposophy may

perhaps as yet have paid little attention to the exercises for perception or the meditations included here, instead basing their work more upon those exercises directed specifically towards a transformation of thinking. That path has certainly been more prominent in anthroposophical tradition since Rudolf Steiner's time. In many lectures and books he himself repeatedly emphasized the path which takes its departure from pure thinking.

However, if we examine his basic work *Knowledge of the Higher Worlds* more closely, a rather different picture emerges. Immediately in the introductory chapter there is mention of a fundamental *feeling* of devotion.[2] Ordinary thinking, and especially critical thinking, must be reined in to a greater degree in this connection. Therefore a relationship with the world founded not on thinking but on perceiving is the subject of the following chapters and of the schooling for meditative work.

The texts selected here, together with other descriptions by Rudolf Steiner, are presented with the aim of bringing these aspects to the fore. The purpose is not to contradict descriptions of a schooling path founded solely on thinking but rather to draw attention to the fact that a path based *exclusively* on thinking cannot be successful without being supported by the aspects of perception, feeling and will. The aspects of perception and feeling are clearly explained in the exercises described in *Knowledge of the Higher Worlds* as being for 'Preparation' and 'Enlightenment'.

In other meditative schooling paths, especially of an eastern character[3] (such as those offered by the Buddhist monk from Vietnam Thich Nhat-Hanh and the American teacher of meditation Jon Kabat-Zinn), the aspect of perception is nowadays usually termed 'mindfulness'. Rudolf Steiner chose to speak of 'attentiveness' and 'dedication' or, combining these two, 'pure perception'. Above all he had the scientific considerations of Goethe in mind. With the meditative exercises in *Knowledge of the Higher Worlds* he was thus emphasizing the western, Rosicrucian, tradition of attentiveness which, however, in its loving focus upon what is perceived does also touch on the eastern path. Hence, in order to show that the western tradition of the Rosicrucian path also involves the eastern aspect of schooling, we have chosen to include the word 'mindfulness' in the title of our collection of texts since it is frequently used with reference to eastern traditions.

In the compilation of meditative exercises contained here, which connect with the perceptive activity of the human being's sensory organs, especially those of seeing and hearing, and which aim to bring about an intensified experience of the breathing process, Rudolf Steiner develops the anthroposophical schooling path as an additional aspect of, or indeed as a counterbalance to, today's increasing intellectualization. In the twenty-first century, over one hundred years after the founding of this path of meditation and knowledge, its value is only now beginning to reveal its full import and scope.

Our present age is characterized by an overestimation of the powers of the intellect and an underestimation of those of perception and feeling. The ubiquitous presence of artificial intelligence in computers, mobile telephones and the internet has led to a worldwide predominance of a specific type of life and attitude founded on the agility of our nervous system which has come to be reflected artificially in the digital media. Conversely, the capacity to feel through the senses is being taken over by a virtual world of perceptions which are no longer physically real. The more these technologies are disseminated, even into the most poverty-stricken regions of our earth, the greater will be the threat to our sensory perceptions and the world of thoughts and feelings connected with them.

In view of the one-sidedness of today's digital civilization, younger individuals now becoming acquainted with anthroposophy will be attracted to the anthroposophical schooling path because it is more congruent with their often more empathetic mode of encountering the world. This is born out by statements made by Rudolf Steiner early in the twentieth century in which he referred to the opening up of new capacities for perceiving the etheric world.[4] However, the development of such capacities came to be massively suppressed by the history of that century. But as the twenty-first century begins, such new faculties of perception are indeed becoming increasingly noticeable, especially among the younger generation.

One might therefore also venture to describe the exercises discussed here as exercises for the faculty of empathy, for it is their aim to render more conscious and more intense the relationship the human being has with the world around him through his organs of sense perception.

Rather than a direct experience of the senses during the process of perceiving, however, what is meant more precisely is a deepening of what arises in the soul in connection with a sensory experience of, for example, a specific plant or a specific sound in nature. As an example of this, Rudolf Steiner quoted the 'sensory and moral' experience of colours described by Goethe and the *after-images* also described by him as sensory experiences. All in all, then, in most of the exercises discussed here we are concerned with a deepening of the after-images of sensory impressions by way of a moral feeling towards those sense-impressions.

As well as in his basic book *Knowledge of the Higher Worlds*, Rudolf Steiner also spoke about the supersensible perception of nature in two wide-ranging lecture cycles: *Spiritual Beings in the Heavenly Bodies and in the Kingdoms of Nature* (CW 136) and *Harmony of the Creative Word* (CW 230). A study of these two cycles in the present context would be well worthwhile.

Meanwhile, the endeavours of a number of authors have resulted in the creation of a great deal of anthroposophical literature focusing on the supersensible perception of nature. This has come to be referred to as 'research into the formative forces'. Among these authors are Dorian Schmidt, Markus Buchmann, Jürgen Strube, Dirk Kruse, Thomas Meyer and Karsten Massei whose numerous publications are highly recommended. The texts from the works of Rudolf Steiner presented here have been chosen specifically to complement the research and suggestions of these authors.

The fact that every artistic experience can be enhanced by the schooling path described here, indeed that all artistic activity is closely bound up with the exercises, is mentioned by Rudolf Steiner at the beginning of the chapter 'Preparation' in *Knowledge of the Higher Worlds*. Thus by their very nature these exercises can be of great interest in connection with all forms of artistic endeavour because they deepen and widen the sensory experience upon which all artistic creativity is founded.

In working with these exercises one is expected to discipline one's thinking in a way that takes seriously the reality and the invisible force of thought. Rather than strengthening it, Rudolf Steiner is more concerned here that clarity and orderliness should be brought into thinking. Who has not many times been aware of thinking as having as much force as a shot from a gun in the physical world? And yet how often have we acted in keeping with this? So in the present volume considerable significance is attached to the moral component expressed in the exercises discussed here as being especially concerned with purifying the life of thought and the life of feeling (Chapter 8).

Our collection begins with a brief quotation from a lecture in which the fundamental quality of reverence is described. This is followed by the exercises given in 1904 and 1905 in the section 'Preparation' in *Knowledge of the Higher Worlds* (Chapter 1). This basic text is then expanded by a description of the fundamental difference between the ancient yoga path and the anthroposophical path. The former aims to approach thinking through an intensification of breathing while the latter seeks to separate the processes of perception and thinking from breathing. This is then followed by three exercises in perception which Rudolf Steiner presented to his audience during lectures given in Helsingfors (Helsinki).

The selection then turns to the important theme of the 'light-soul-process' (Chapter 2). Here Rudolf Steiner describes the onward development of the ancient Indian path of yoga which enabled the individual to deepen his relationship with the world through regulating the physical process of breathing. However, as the I of the human being developed, his relationship with his surroundings, having previously been regulated by means of the breathing process, was now more influenced by his sensory awareness.

Today, therefore, rather than emphasizing the physical process of breathing it is more important to pay attention to the soul-spiritual breathing process which comes about between perception through the senses and perception through thinking. Thus Steiner also spoke of a *new* yoga path which relates to the processes taking place in our consciousness nowadays.

This new yoga path consists of a breathing of spirit and soul. First one *concentrates one's entire attention* on an object, examining and observing every detail (inhalation). Then one *dedicates* oneself utterly to the impression gained through the enhanced attentiveness and *meditates* it (exhalation). In the first step, of exact observation, thinking is reined in and remains in the realm of registering what is being observed. In the second step, that of actual meditation, thinking begins to metamorphose, taking on the form of a receptacle opening itself to receive the actual spiritual content of the meditation. Here the two trees mentioned earlier, the Tree of Knowledge and the Tree of Life, begin to fructify and permeate one another.

Through the depictions which follow the descriptions of the 'light-soul-process', it becomes clear that Rudolf Steiner is speaking not merely of a thinking that is free of the body and unfettered by the brain, but of pure perception which is free of the body and disengaged from the brain. Steiner also discusses this in a number of instances from the point of view of physiology by describing the organism of our senses as having a breathing relationship with the external world (Chapters 3 and 4).

The other exercises aimed at enlightenment given in *Knowledge of the Higher Worlds* are also directed towards pure perception. They are supplemented in this volume by further exercises from lectures given later (Chapters 5 and 7).

As already mentioned, Rudolf Steiner links these exercises with the Rosicrucianism of Goethe.[5] It was the aim of historical Rosicrucianism to comprehend and transform the sense-perceptible world of matter and of nature in a manner that would transcend intellectual thinking. In former times this involved renouncing intellectual thinking. It was Rudolf Steiner's achievement, in the present time, to link ancient Rosicrucianism with a form of spiritualized thinking that can be combined successfully with what is nowadays a generally comprehensible way of thinking.

Thus the exercises in this volume, which are concerned with the sense-perceptible world and pure perception, have to be founded on the refined, pure thinking which Rudolf Steiner always postulates, as for example in his pivotal depiction of pure perception in *The Boundaries of Natural Science* (see Chapter 6). The art of the schooling path depicted here is revealed, especially in the moment when perception is being practised, in the way thinking must be reined in so that the meditant can devote himself entirely to the sensory process and the resulting after-images. Only then can the 'light-soul-process' become a genuine 'light-soul-breathing'. Whereas in the ancient yoga tradition it was a matter of restraint in physical breathing, in this new yoga path it is the thinking which has to be reined in so that the perception can become more profound.

By means of this way of breathing, which might be termed a new yoga path, the soul gains new, hitherto unfamiliar feelings and thoughts, which previously only flitted past unconsciously. In this way the increasingly overheated speed of the processes of intelligence, caused by the digitization of civilization, can be countered by an element of conscious *slowing down* of the breathing process that comes about unconsciously between perceiving and thinking in the deeper recesses of the unconscious. Whereas, during the process of ego development, the old yoga path proceeded inwards from the outside through breathing, the new yoga path now sets out along the path of perception from the newly created ego-consciousness towards the external world so that it may there merge with it in loving devotion.

Through the deepening within the soul of the feelings and thoughts that accompany perception through the senses, the soul arrives at a perception of a supersensible world which is immediately adjacent to the world revealed by the senses. Steiner's statements quoted in Chapters 3 and 4 tell us that our senses are part and parcel of the etheric world, that supersensible world with which the human being is bound up through his senses. It is solely his intellect, which is bound up with his brain, that initially prevents him from becoming aware of the supersensible. As Goethe said, 'There is no need to look behind the phenomena; they themselves are the doctrine.' That is why his way of perceiving in the natural sciences became the example to be followed along Steiner's path of knowledge. As the exercises show, this path leads to a recognition and a deepening of our perceptions of the world. Thus Steiner addressed himself to a theme which had already been known within Christian mysticism as the 'conversation with the goddess Natura'. He deepened this so that it became a modern science which can be further developed spiritually (Chapter 9).

Finally, the 'seven conditions' (Chapter 10) described in *Knowledge of the Higher Worlds* show in this connection how such an attitude to everyday life can come to form a continuous breathing process which helps the individual to build a healthy, loving relationship with nature and with the human beings all around him. In all this Rudolf Steiner knew himself to be in touch with the Archangel Michael, the being who had formerly been in charge of the original cosmic intelligence. Michael is watching over human evolution with great concern inasmuch as what was once cosmic intelligence has become human intelligence which is now increasingly threatening to become an intelligence dominated by machines. That is why Rudolf Steiner describes as 'Michael's Mission' the path depicted here as a new yoga oriented towards the processes of sense perception. Those who are true to Michael will cultivate love towards the external world through developing 'light-soul-breathing'. Through this new breathing the individual will increasingly be enabled to unite in love with nature and with his fellow human beings.

Andreas Neider

1. The Preparation

We may also ask ourselves:[6] What is it that develops in the consciousness soul, without its cooperation, which accords with the urges and desires of the <u>sentient</u> soul? What develops in it that corresponds with human aptitudes so that the human being can only develop it to a lesser degree if it does not come about as the result of a predisposition? There is something which rises up out of the intellectual or mind soul into the consciousness soul; thinking. It is the strength, the cleverness of thinking. The consciousness soul can only be developed if the human being becomes a thinker; for the self-conscious soul must have knowledge, knowledge of the world and of itself. It can only be developed by means of the highest instrument of knowledge, namely thinking. With regard to the external world, the world of the senses, it is external feeling and perception that give us knowledge. In external feeling and perception, in what is all around us, we have the stimulus which shows us how to know about the external sense-perceptible world. This also involves putting oneself at the disposal of that world rather than being obtuse towards it. It is the external, sense-perceptible world itself which stimulates us; through observing it we can satisfy our external desire and thirst for knowledge.

Things are different with regard to what is to be discussed again and again here in these lectures about spiritual science. Knowing about what is <u>not sense-perceptible</u>, namely the supersensible, is different. Initially the supersensible is nonexistent as far as we are concerned. If we want to bring it into the realm of our knowledge, if we want to fill our consciousness soul with it, then, since the object of what we want to know is not externally present, we need to find an incentive from within; the impulse must come from within ourselves. This impulse which comes from within must stimulate our thinking, it must stream through our thinking and intermingle with it. When an impulse of this kind is to emanate from the soul, it can only emanate from those forces which are already within it, and these are feeling and will, in addition to thinking.

If our thinking does not allow itself to be stimulated by those other two, then it cannot be compelled to enter into a supersensible world. This does not mean to say that what is supersensible is nothing but a feeling. The point is that feeling and will within the human being must be what leads him to the supersensible. What leads us is not what we are seeking. The human being must seek for the supersensible world because initially it is unknown to him. From the outset he must have feeling and will from within himself as his guide. So what attributes must feeling and will adopt if they are to become our guides into the spiritual world, the supersensible world?

At first glance it would be quite possible for someone to object to the supposition that feeling can guide us towards knowledge. But there is a simple consideration which shows us that feeling must in every way be what guides us in our search for knowledge. When we take the matter of knowledge seriously we have to admit that of course we must proceed in a logical way in our search for it and that we must be permeated and guided by logic. Those things which become knowledge for us must be proved logically. We use logic as an instrument by means of which we prove what we obtain as knowledge.

But if logic is this instrument, what, then, is there which can prove the logic? In answer to this we have to say that logic itself is the means of its own proof. But before proving logic by means of logic it must at least be possible to enfold it in feeling. Logical thinking can in the first instance not be proved through logical thinking but only through feeling. All logic is initially proved by feeling, by the human soul's infallible feeling for truth. This classic example shows us that logic itself is founded on feeling, that feeling provides the foundation for thinking, and that feeling provides the impulse by means of which thinking is proven. What must the nature of this feeling be if it is to provide not only the impulse for thinking as such but also for thinking about worlds which are initially unknown to human beings, worlds which they are initially unable to comprehend?

The characteristic that feeling must adopt if it is to lead to the unknown must be a power which strives from within to find something unfamiliar, something about which one as yet has no knowledge. If the human soul is striving to discover something different, if this human soul is striving to embrace something with feeling, that feeling is known by the name of love. One can feel love for something with which one is familiar, and we must indeed love much with which we are familiar in this world. But since love is a feeling, and since feeling must provide the basis for thinking in the widest sense, we must realize—if something supersensible is to be discovered through thinking—that the supersensible which is as yet unknown to us must initially be embraced by feeling before it can be embraced by thinking.

What this means is that it must be possible—and unbiased observation has proved that this is so—for love to be developed for what is unknown, namely for the supersensible, before it can be comprehended through thinking. Love for what is supersensible, before one is able to penetrate it with the light of thinking, is possible, indeed necessary. And our will, also, can fill itself with a power that streams forth towards the unknown supersensible before thinking can approach it. Dedication to the unknown is the attribute of the will by means of which we desire to perform in our will the aims and purposes of the unknown prior to being able to grasp it with the light of our thinking. So our will can develop dedication to the unknown and our feeling can develop love towards the unknown.

And when dedication of the will to the unknown and also love towards the unknown—when these two unite, then, in their union, what is best described as reverence arises. And when reverence gives us discernment of and insight into the mutual fructification of love for the unknown and dedication to the unknown, then this reverence can provide the impetus which leads us into the unknown in a way that enables our thinking to take hold of it. So reverence becomes the teacher of our consciousness soul. When our consciousness soul searches for something that is initially hidden from it one can also speak of reverence even in everyday life.

When we are confronted with something unknown, something we are as yet incapable of grasping even though it is an outward reality, then we can speak of approaching this unknown element in love and dedication. Our consciousness soul will never attain any knowledge even about something external if we do not approach this external thing with love and dedication, for our soul fails to notice things which it does not approach with love and dedication or, in other words, with reverence. This is our guide to knowledge, to knowledge about the unknown. This is what love and dedication are, even in ordinary life; but this is especially what they are when our concern is directed towards the super-sensible.

(*28 October 1909*)

Preparation[7]

Preparation involves a very definite cultivation of the life of feeling and of thought, through which the 'body' of soul and spirit becomes equipped with higher instruments of sense and organs of activity, in the same way that forces of nature have equipped the physical body with organs moulded out of non-specific living matter.

The first step is taken by directing the attention of the soul to certain processes taking place in the world around us. Such processes are, on the one hand, life that is budding, growing, thriving and, on the other, all phenomena of fading, decay, withering. A person can see all this going on at once wherever he looks, and in the nature of things it evokes feelings and thoughts in him. But in ordinary circumstances he pays too little attention to these thoughts and feelings. He hurries too quickly from one impression to the next. The essential point is that he should fix his attention intently and consciously upon them. Wherever he observes a quite definite blossoming and thriving, he should banish everything else from his soul and for a short time give himself up entirely to *this one* impression. He will soon convince himself that a feeling which would previously have merely flitted through his soul now acquires a strong and energetic force. He must then allow his feelings to reverberate quietly within himself, while maintaining perfect inner calm. He must shut himself off from the rest of the outer world and follow only what his soul has to say about the phenomena of blossoming and thriving.

It must not be assumed that much progress can be made if the *senses* are blunted. First look at things in the world as keenly and precisely as you possibly can. *Only then* give yourself up to the feeling and the thought arising in the soul. What is important is that attention should be directed with perfect inner equilibrium upon *both* activities. If you achieve the necessary tranquillity and if you surrender yourself to what arises in the soul, then, after a time, the following will be *experienced*. Thoughts and feelings of a new character, previously unknown, will be noticed rising up in the soul. Indeed, the more often the attention is turned alternately in this way upon something that is growing, blossoming and thriving and then upon something that is fading and dying, the more animated will these feelings become. And just as natural forces build the eyes and ears of the physical body out of living substance, so will the organs of clairvoyance be built out of the feelings and thoughts thus evoked. A quite definite form of feeling is connected with growth and development, and another, equally definite, with what is fading and dying. But this will come about only if an effort is made to cultivate these feelings in the way indicated.

It is possible to describe approximately what these feelings are like. A clear mental picture of them is within the reach of everyone who has these inner experiences. Those who have often turned their attention to the process of growing, blossoming and thriving will feel something *distantly resembling* the experience of a sunrise. And the process of fading and dying will evoke an experience comparable in the same way to the slow rising of the moon over the horizon. These feelings are two forces which, when properly nurtured and developed to an ever-increasing pitch, lead to significant spiritual results. A new world opens up for those who systematically and deliberately surrender themselves again and again to such feelings. The soul-world, the so-called astral plane, begins to dawn before one. Growth and decay no longer remain facts that make vague impressions on one. They form themselves into spiritual lines and figures of which one had previously known nothing. And these lines and figures differ according to the phenomena they represent. A blossoming flower, a growing animal or a dying tree will each conjure up a very definite form before the soul. The soul-world (the astral plane) slowly spreads out before one. These lines and figures have nothing arbitrary about them. Two pupils who have reached the appropriate stage of development will always see the same lines and figures in connection with the same phenomena. Just as a round table will be seen as round by two persons with normal sight and not as round by one and square by the other, so at the sight of a blossom will the same spiritual figure present itself to two souls. And just as the forms of plants and animals are described in ordinary natural history, so does anyone versed in occult science describe the spiritual forms of the processes of growth and decay according to species and genus.

If the pupil has progressed so far that he can perceive the spiritual forms of phenomena which are also physically visible to his outer sight, he will then not be far from the stage of seeing things which have no physical existence and must therefore remain entirely hidden (occult) for anyone who has not received instruction in occult science.

It should be emphasized that the occult investigator must not become lost in speculation as to the *meaning* of one thing or another. By such intellectualizing he merely diverts himself from the right path. He should look out on the world with fresh, healthy senses and a keen power of observation, and then surrender to his feelings. He should not try through intellectual speculation to determine what the things mean, but should rather allow the things themselves to tell him.[*]

A further important matter is *orientation*—as occult science calls it—in the higher worlds. This is achieved when the individual is permeated through and through with a conscious realization that feelings and thoughts are *veritable realities*, just as are chairs and tables in the physical world of

---

[*] It should be remarked that *artistic* feeling, coupled with a quiet, introspective nature, is the best preliminary condition for the development of spiritual faculties. Artistic feeling pierces through the surface of things, and by so doing reaches their secrets.

the senses. In the soul-world and in the world of thoughts, feelings and thoughts work upon each other just as physical objects do in the physical world. As long as anyone is not vividly imbued with this awareness he will not believe that a wrong thought he harbours may have as devastating an effect upon other thoughts, in the realm of thoughts, as the effect of a random bullet has on the physical objects it hits. Such an individual may perhaps never allow himself to perform a physically visible act that he regards as senseless; yet he will not shrink from harbouring wrong thoughts or feelings, because these appear to him to be harmless for the rest of the world. In occult science, however, progress is possible only when as much care is given to thoughts and feelings as to steps taken in the physical world. If someone sees a wall before him, he does not attempt to dash through it; he turns aside. He conforms with the laws of the physical world.

There are such laws, too, for the world of feeling and thought, only they cannot impose themselves on man from without. They must flow out of the life of one's own soul. This is achieved if one forbids oneself at all times to harbour wrong thoughts and feelings. All arbitrary flitting hither-and-thither in thought, all capricious play of fancy, all fortuitous ebb and flow of emotion, must be forbidden. By observing this rule, nobody becomes poverty-stricken in feeling. On the contrary, if the inner life is regulated in this way one will soon find oneself becoming rich in feeling and in genuine imaginativeness. Petty emotionalism and frivolous flights of fancy are replaced by significant emotions and fruitful thoughts. Such feelings and thoughts teach us how to *orientate* ourselves in the spiritual world. We establish the right relationship to the things of that world, and this has a definite effect. Just as we, as physical human beings, find our way between physical things, so now does our path lead us between the phenomena of *growing* and *withering* which we have already come to know in the way described above. Then we follow all processes of growing and dying in a way which promotes our own advancement as well as that of the world.

The pupil must also give further care to cultivating the world of *sound*. He must discriminate between the sounds produced by anything described as being *lifeless* (for example, a falling object, a bell or a musical instrument) and the sounds that come from a living creature (an animal or a human being). Someone who hears the sound of a bell may associate a feeling of pleasure with it; someone who hears the cry of an animal will discern in the sound, besides his own feeling, the expression of an inner experience of the animal, whether of pleasure or of pain. It is with the latter category of sounds that the pupil must set to work. He must concentrate his whole attention on the fact that the sound tells him of something which is foreign to his own soul, and he must immerse himself in this foreign element. He must unite his own feeling inwardly with the pain or pleasure of which the sound tells him. He must be beyond caring whether *for him* the sound is pleasant or unpleasant, agreeable or disagreeable; his soul must be imbued only with what is going on in the being from whom the sound emanates. Anyone who carries out such exercises with method and deliberation will acquire the faculty of blending, as it were, with the being from whom the sound is emanating. To cultivate his life in this way will be easier for a person sensitive to music than for one who is unmusical. But let no one believe that a sense for music can be a substitute for this cultivation. The pupil of occult science must learn to respond in this way to the *whole of nature*.

By this means a new faculty will take root in the world of feeling and thought. Through her resounding tones, the whole of nature begins to whisper her secrets to the pupil. What he has previously experienced as incomprehensible noise will become an expressive *language of nature* herself. And whereas he had previously heard only sounds from the so-called lifeless world, he is now aware of a new language of the soul. If he makes further progress in this cultivation of his feelings, he will realize that he can hear things of which he knew nothing hitherto. He begins to *hear with the soul*.

Something more still has to be added in order that the highest point attainable in this particular field of experience may be reached. Of very special importance for the pupil's development is the way in which he *listens* to others when they are speaking. He must accustom himself to do this in such a way that, while listening, his own inner self is absolutely *silent*. When someone expresses an opinion and another listens, agreement or contradiction will generally be set astir in the listener. Many will also feel impelled to voice their agreement or, more especially, their disagreement. The pupil must silence all such inner agreement or disagreement. It is not a matter of suddenly altering his mode of life in such a way that he strives to bring about this inner silence all the time. He will have to begin by doing so in particular cases, deliberately chosen. Then, quite slowly and by degrees, as of itself, this entirely new kind of listening will become habitual.

In spiritual research this is systematically practised. The pupils are enjoined to listen at certain times, by way of practice, to the most contradictory views and to silence in themselves all positive agreement and, more especially, all adverse criticism. The point is to silence not only all intellectual judgement, but also all feelings of displeasure and denial, or agreement. The pupil must always watch himself carefully to see whether such feelings, even when not on the surface, may not still be present in the inmost core of his soul. He must listen, for example, to the utterance of those who in one respect or another are inferior to him, while yet suppressing *every* feeling of superiority or of possessing greater knowledge. It is useful for everyone to listen in this way to children, for even the wisest can learn immeasurably from children.

Thus the pupil comes to listen to the words of others quite *selflessly*, while completely shutting out his own personality, with its opinions and trends of feeling. When he has trained himself to listen without criticism, when even the most preposterous statement is made in his presence, he learns gradually to merge himself into the being of another. Then he hears *through* the words into the very soul of the other. It is through assiduous practice of this kind that sound becomes for the first time the right means for perceiving the soul and spirit. Certainly this requires the most rigorous self-discipline, but it leads to a lofty goal. When these exercises are practised in connection with the others that have been indicated concerning the sounds of the world of nature, a new sense of hearing develops in the soul. The soul is now able to become aware of communications from the spiritual world which are not expressed in sounds perceptible to the physical ear. Perception of the 'inner word' awakens. Truths from the spiritual world gradually reveal themselves to the pupil. He hears himself addressed spiritually.*

All higher truths are attained through such 'perception of the inner word'. And what we hear from the lips of a genuine spiritual investigator has been expressed by him in this way. But this does not mean that it is unnecessary to acquaint oneself with the literature of occult science before being able to hear this 'inner word' oneself. On the contrary, the reading of this literature and listening to the teachings given by occult science are themselves means of attaining personal knowledge. Every sentence of occult science is able to direct the mind to the point that must be reached if the soul is to make true progress. To all that has here been said must be added the zealous study of what the occult investigators communicate to the world. In all occult training such study belongs to the stage of Preparation. And anyone who might try all kinds of other methods would reach no goal if he did not absorb the teachings resulting from occult investigation. For because these teachings are drawn from the living 'inner word', from living perception of the 'inner word', they themselves have spiritual life. They are not merely words— they are living powers. And while you follow the words of one versed in occult science, while you read a book that originates

---

* It is only to one who through selfless listening can become inwardly receptive in the real sense, in quietude and unmoved by any personal opinion or feeling, that the higher beings of whom occult science tells can speak. So long as a person directs any opinion, any feeling, against what is to be heard, the beings of the spiritual world will remain silent.

from genuine inner experience, powers are at work in your soul which make you clairvoyant, just as the forces of nature have created your eyes and ears out of living substance.

(*Knowledge of the Higher Worlds*, 1904/1905)

It cannot be the task of today's human beings[8] to find their way into the spiritual worlds in this manner, which was appropriate for bygone days. The human being of today should not find his way upwards into the spiritual worlds via the detour of breathing; he should follow a rather more soul-filled path, the path of thinking, to find his way upwards into spiritual worlds. So today it is right that the individual should enter on his own initiative into meditation, into bringing his thoughts and inner images together in, as it were, a musical coherence rather than a merely logical coherence. Meditation today is always an experience in thinking, a transition of one thought into the next, a transition of one mental image into another.

Whereas a yogi in ancient Indian times made the transition from one way of breathing to another, a human being today must endeavour to enter with his whole soul in a living way into, for example, the colour red. He remains within the realm of thought. And then he moves on into the colour blue. He follows the rhythm: red-blue; blue-red; red-blue. This is a rhythm of thinking in a much more living way than merely following a logical sequence of thoughts.

When an individual practises such exercises for a sufficient length of time—just as was also necessary for a yogi in ancient times—when the individual experiences the momentum, the rhythm, the inwardly qualitative alternation red-blue, blue-red, light-dark, dark-light, in short, when he follows instructions such as those included in my book *Knowledge of the Higher Worlds*, when, rather than pausing in his thinking in order to drive his breath into his nerve-sense processes but instead makes the nerve-sense processes themselves his starting point, taking them into an internal impetus and rhythm and into a qualitative rearrangement, then he achieves the very opposite of what the yogi of old achieved. In some measure the yogi of old conflated the thought process with the breathing process. We today, however, endeavour to loosen even further the final link between the breathing process and the thought process, which is anyway deeply unconscious. When in today's ordinary consciousness you think about your natural surroundings, your ideas are most certainly not held in a purely nerve-sense process; breathing is also still involved. You do still think while your breathing continuously flows and weaves through your nerve-sense process.

All meditative exercises today aim at separating thinking entirely from the breathing process. This is not the same as extricating it from rhythm as such; instead one separates it from a rhythm which is internal. Thus one gradually combines thinking with an external rhythm. By extricating thinking from the rhythm of breathing—which is the aim of our present-day meditations—one in some measure allows thinking to flow into the rhythm of the external world, whereas the yogi returned to his own rhythm. Nowadays the individual returns to the rhythm of the external world. Read the very first exercises I gave in *Knowledge of the Higher*

Worlds, where I show how one should follow, let's say, the burgeoning and growing of a plant. The meditation aims to extricate the idea or the thinking from the breath so that it enters instead into the growth forces of the plant itself.

It is intended that thinking should enter into the rhythm which permeates the external world. When thinking truly breaks free in this way from the functions of the body, when it extricates itself from the breath, when it gradually unites with the external rhythm, it is at this moment that it immerses itself not in sensory perceptions, not in the sensory properties of things but rather in their spiritual aspect.

When you look at a plant you see that it is green and has red flowers. Your eyes tell you this. And then you think about it with your understanding. It is on this that our ordinary consciousness lives. But we develop a different kind of consciousness when we extricate our thinking from our breathing and unite it instead with what is outside ourselves. This kind of thinking learns to vibrate along with the plant as it grows and as it unfolds its flower—as in the rose, for example, the green colour goes over into the red. This vibrates outwards into the spiritual realm which underlies every single thing in the external world.

So you see, this is the difference between modern meditation and the exercises of the yogi of olden times. Of course much lies in between these; I refer merely to the two extremes. And now the following comes about when the individual finds his way livingly into this external rhythm.

The yogi immersed himself in his own breathing process. He became absorbed within himself. In this way he found himself like a memory. He as it were remembered what he had been formerly, before descending to the earth. We, with our soul, we extricate ourselves from our body. We unite ourselves with what lives outside in the rhythm, with what lives in the spirit. In this way we now look at what we were before we descended to the earth.

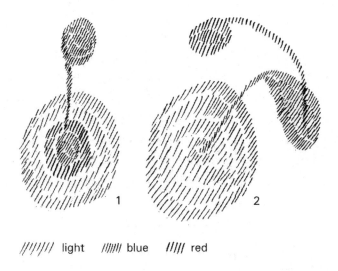

////// light   ///// blue   ///// red

So you see, this is the difference. Let me make a drawing of it. If this was the yogi [Drawing 1, light], he developed a strong feeling of his I [red]. With this feeling of his I he remembered what he had been before descending to the earth, where he had been within an environment of spirit and soul [blue]. The stream of remembering moved backwards.

If this here is the modern spiritual researcher [Drawing 2, light], he brings about a process by which he departs from his body [blue] and thus lives in the rhythm of the external world and now looks as though at an external object [red] towards what he previously was before coming down to earth.

Thus, in olden times, perception of one's pre-birth condition was something like a memory. And in the present time, perception of one's pre-birth condition, if it is correctly developed, involves seeing what one was formerly [red]. That is the difference.

(*27 May 1922*)

Now I must show you why it is possible to claim[9] that an ether or life body, or indeed actually an ether- or life-world, a multiplicity, a diversity of differentiated beings, is to be found beyond our physical nature. I can explain quite simply how it is possible to come into contact with that world: we can increasingly come into contact with that ether- or life-world which lies behind physical nature by developing moral feelings for the world all around us.

What do we mean by developing moral feelings about the world? As a start, we can direct our gaze upwards to the expanses of the universe out of which the blue of the heavens approaches us. We take for granted that we are doing this on a day when there is not even the smallest cloud in the sky, not the flimsiest white shimmer interrupting the sky's blueness. We take for granted that we are gazing in every direction into the blue of the sky expanding above us. It is not a matter of whether we consider this to be the actual situation in a physical sense. It is first and foremost a matter of the impression we gain from the blue sky as it unfolds above us.

Let us assume that we are able to abandon ourselves intensively to the blue of the sky for a long, long time and also in a way that enables us to forget everything we know in life and everything which normally surrounds us in our lives. Let us assume that we can for a while forget all external impressions, all memories, all our worries about life, all of life's tribulations, and simply abandon ourselves to the single impression of the blueness of the sky. What I am describing can be experienced by every human soul if only an appropriate effort is made; what I am describing can become a universal human experience.

So now imagine a human soul looking all around at nothing but the blue of the heavens when that blue ceases to be blue, when blueness is no longer visible, when nothing more can be seen which in any human language might be described as blue. If, when for us the blue ceases to be blue, we at that moment turn our attention to our own soul, we shall notice within it a mood which is quite specific. The blue, as it were, disappears and an infinitude opens up before us; and into this infinitude a specific mood of soul, a quite specific feeling, a quite specific sensibility of our soul proceeds to pour into the void which arises where previously all was blue. And if we want to give a name to that sensibility of our soul which proceeds to flow into all those infinite distances, there is only one word which can describe it, and that is piety; our soul feels ardently pious towards such an infinity. All the religious feelings experienced throughout human evolution have at their core a single nuance which is what I here mean by piety. The impression gained from the blue dome of the heavens is one of pious, religious devotion and morality. Those blue expanses generate a moral feeling in our soul, and when the blue disappears there arises in our soul a moral feeling towards the external world.

Let us now turn our attention to a different sensibility, a

different mood in which we can morally approach external nature. Let us look at nature as the trees come into leaf and the meadows turn green. Let us now pay attention to the green that spreads across the land and the trees. Once again we shall ignore all the external impressions coming towards us and now devote ourselves entirely to all the green that meets us in external nature.

If we are able to immerse ourselves entirely in all the green springing up around us we shall reach a point when the green disappears, just as previously the blue of the blueness disappeared. Once again we cannot speak of a colour spreading out before our eyes—and let me remind you that I am speaking of something which all those can experience who do what is necessary—but rather we find that our soul gains a singular feeling. It feels: Now I understand what I am experiencing when I imagine, when I think, when a thought rises up in me, when I have an inward perception! Only now do I comprehend this through being taught by the green sprouting up all around me. I am taught by external nature to comprehend what is inmost in my soul once that external nature has disappeared and left me with a moral impression. The green of the plants tells me what I should sense within myself when my soul is blessed with the ability to think thoughts and have perceptions. Thus, once again, an impression from external nature is transformed into a moral feeling.

Or suppose we turn our attention to a white expanse of snow. This too, as with the blue of the sky and the green of the earth's vegetation, can bring about a moral feeling towards all that can be described as the manifestation of

substance in the world. Only when our view of the white
covering of snow has disappeared so that we can feel the
whiteness itself, which then also disappears, can we reach an
understanding of the substance which fills the world. Then it
is that we feel the substance weaving and flowing in the
world.

In this way all external impressions gained through seeing
can be transformed into moral impressions, and in the same
way impressions gained through hearing can be transformed
into moral feelings. Suppose we hear a note and then its
octave. If, on hearing this chord of a keynote with its octave,
we can develop a mood of soul in which all else is forgotten
while we devote out attention to the keynote with its octave,
we shall, even though two notes are sounding, no longer hear
them; by turning our attention away from them we shall find
instead a moral feeling in our soul. We then begin to gain a
spiritual comprehension of what we experience when we
entertain a wish upon which our thinking works. The con-
sonance of a wish with our thinking, of a thought with our
desire, in the way they live in the human soul, this is felt by
the soul through the sound of a keynote with its octave.

It would be possible for us to let all kinds of sense
impressions work upon us in this way. By then allowing
whatever we perceive in nature through our senses to disappear, we clear away the sense-perceptible covering, thus
everywhere revealing moral feelings of sympathy and antip-
athy. If we become accustomed in this way to blanking out
whatever we see with our eyes, what we hear with our ears,
what we take hold of with our hands, what our understanding, tethered as it is to our brain, comprehends, and if

we then nevertheless continue to confront the world, then something will begin to work within us which is more profound than the power of sight in our eyes, than the power of hearing in our ears, than the power of understanding in the thinking of our brain.

For then we shall be meeting the world with a greater depth of our own being. Then the wide expanses of infinity work on us in a way which bathes us in a religious mood. Then the plants' green covering works on us in a way which enables us to feel how we are beginning to bloom and flower inwardly. Then the snow's white covering works on us in the way it gives us an understanding of what matter is, what substance is in the world. Then something, something which is more profound within us than what we usually apply, begins to grasp the world. And in this way we reach greater depths in the world than is otherwise the case. The external veil of nature is, as it were, drawn aside so that we may then enter into a world which usually lies hidden behind that outer veil.

Just as we enter into the ether or life body when we look beyond the human being's physical body, so in this way do we enter a realm where gradually a multitude of beings reveal themselves, those beings who have their life and activity beyond the mineral realm and beyond the realm of animals and plants. Gradually, and after a while, the etheric world begins to open up to us in all its differentiated detail.

(*3 April 1912*)

2. The Light-Soul-Process

What matters here[10] is the fact that an effort, a conscious effort, must be made to win back what has been lost. In other words we must once more grasp something within the human being which also exists in the external world; the two are intermingled. The fifth post-Atlantean epoch must strive for this. It must be the endeavour of the fifth post-Atlantean epoch to search for something within us in which an external process is also taking place.

No doubt you will recall that I pointed to this important fact in my recent article in the journal *Die Soziale Zukunft* ('The Social Future') where I hinted that these things are important for our social life. What I clearly stated was that something must be found within the human being which he also recognizes as a process belonging to the world. Living as we do in this present age, we cannot achieve this by reverting to the culture of yoga; that is now past. You see, the breathing process as such has changed. Obviously, this cannot be proven clinically. Nevertheless, the human being's breathing process has been different since the third post-Atlantean cultural age. Put bluntly, one could say that during the third post-Atlantean cultural age the human being breathed soul, whereas now he breathes air. It is not solely our conceptions that have become materialistic; reality itself has lost its soul.

Please do not regard what I am now saying as something insignificant. Just think how significant it is that the reality in which humanity now lives has changed to such an extent that the air we now breathe is different from what it was four thousand years ago. It is not solely human consciousness that has changed. This is not the only thing. Soul used to live in the very atmosphere of the earth. The air was the soul. But that is not the case now, or rather it is the case now but in a different way. The spiritual beings of elemental nature, about whom I spoke yesterday, do indeed enter into you; you can inhale them if you practise yoga breathing. But what was possible in normal breathing three thousand years ago can no longer be achieved artificially. That it is achievable is the great illusion of those in the East.

What I want to mention now is a definite description of reality. The ensoulment of the air which belongs to human beings no longer exists. That is why those beings (I am inclined to call them anti-Michaelic beings) about whom I spoke yesterday are able to enter into the air and then via the air into human beings. That is how they enter into humanity, as I described yesterday. And we can only drive them out by today replacing the yoga type of practice with the correct practice. We have to be clear about the fact that we must strive for this correct way of doing things. But we can only strive for this correct way when we become conscious of a much more delicate relationship of the human being with the external world, so that with regard to our ether body something can come about which enters ever increasingly into our consciousness, in a similar way to our breathing process.

In our breathing process we inhale fresh air full of oxygen and exhale useless air full of carbon, and a process similar to this takes place with all our perceptions through our senses. Suppose you see something. Let's take a simple example.

You see a flame. As you look at the flame something comes about which can be compared, although it is much more delicate, with breathing in. Then close your eyes (you can do something similar with any of your senses); close your eyes and an after-image of the flame appears which gradually changes, just as Goethe described—it fades.[11] Apart from the purely physiological aspect of this process of receiving the impression of light and of the way it subsequently fades, it is also the human being's ether body which is very thoroughly involved. Something very, very significant is involved in this process, and that is the aspect of the soul which three thousand years ago was inhaled and exhaled together with the air. We must now learn in a similar way to comprehend how the process of perceiving with the senses is also filled with the soul element, just as three thousand years ago the process of breathing was perceived.

There is a link between this and the fact that three thousand years ago human beings lived in what might be described as a kind of culture of the night. It was out of night-time dreams that Yahweh made himself known through his prophets. Nowadays we must cultivate the subtleties of our relationship with the world in such a way that in addition to perceiving through our senses we also experience something spiritual. With every ray of light, with every sound, with every sensation of warmth, in the way these fade away, we must ensure that our soul interacts with the world; and this interaction with our soul must become something that has significance for us. And we can also support ourselves in achieving this.

I have pointed out to you that the Mystery of Golgotha

took place during the fourth post-Atlantean period, the period, to be precise, which began with the year 747 BC and ended in AD 1413. The Mystery of Golgotha took place in the first third of that period. However, it was initially through the final stages of the old way of thinking, the old culture, that people found the ability to comprehend the Mystery of Golgotha. But it is now important for the manner of comprehending the Mystery of Golgotha to become thoroughly renewed. The old manner of comprehending the Mystery of Golgotha is no longer appropriate. It is no longer adequate for this task. Many attempts to make human thinking capable of comprehending the Mystery of Golgotha have proved to be no longer capable of reaching up to the Mystery of Golgotha.

You see, everything that takes place externally, materially, also possesses an aspect belonging to the spirit and soul. And everything taking place spiritually, or through the soul, also has an external, physical aspect. The air belonging to earth became deprived of its soul, so that human beings no longer breathed air which was originally filled with soul, and this has had a significant spiritual effect on the evolution of humanity. We read at the beginning of the Old Testament: 'And with His breath God breathed the living soul into the human being.' Having received in his soul the living breath to which he was originally related, the human being gained an awareness of the soul's pre-existence, of its existence prior to its descent into a physical body through birth, or through conception. And in the same measure as the breathing process lost its soul-filled element, the human being also lost his awareness of his pre-existence prior to birth. Even when

Aristotle appeared during that fourth post-Atlantean period it was no longer possible for human comprehension to grasp the phenomenon of the soul's pre-existence. It was no longer possible.

Historically we find ourselves confronting the strange fact of the most significant event ever, the Christ Event, entering into earthly evolution at a point when humanity must first gain in maturity before being able to comprehend it. Human beings still possess the ancient remnants of comprehension by means of which they can catch the shining rays of the Mystery of Golgotha. But then they lose this capacity, and dogmatism becomes ever more removed from any comprehension of the Mystery of Golgotha. The Church forbids any belief in pre-existence. This is not because pre-existence cannot be linked with the Mystery of Golgotha. It came about on account of the air becoming void of soul forces, so that the human capacity to comprehend pre-existence waned. Pre-existence disappeared from head-consciousness. When we have regained an understanding of how the feelings of our senses are filled with soul, then we shall once again have found a cross-over point; and in this cross-over point we shall grasp the human will as it streams up out of the third level of consciousness, as I have been explaining during these talks. This is where we shall also find the subjective-objective which Goethe was also seeking with such fervour.

Then we shall discover, delicately at first, how remarkable is the human being's relationship, through his senses, with the external world. The idea that the external world simply works upon us and that we then merely react to it is crude and unsubtle. All this stuff that people talk about amounts to no more than crude waffle. The reality is as follows. A soul process goes inwards from the outside and is then grasped by the deeply subconscious inner soul process. Thus the processes overlap. World thoughts work in upon us from the outside while the human will works outwards from within. Thus human will and world thoughts cross over at this crossing point just as once upon a time, in breathing, the objective crossed over with the subjective. We must learn to feel how our will works through our eyes and how the activity of the senses does indeed mingle quietly with passivity whereby the thoughts of the world cross over with the will of humanity. It is this new yoga will which we must develop. And from this we shall then gain something resembling what three thousand years ago human beings received through the process of breathing. Our understanding must become far more filled with soul and with spirit.

Goethe's world-view strove to comprehend such things. Goethe wanted to recognize the pure phenomenon, which he called the archetypal phenomenon. He included in this only what works upon the human being in the external world as such, without any interference from luciferic thoughts arising in the head itself. He regarded such thoughts as merely the link between the phenomena. What Goethe was seeking was not the law of nature but the archetypal phenomenon. That is what is significant for him.

Turning now to this pure phenomenon, this archetypal phenomenon, we have in the external world something which enables us to detect how our will unfolds when we look at the external world. When this comes about we shall be able to approach something which is objective-subjective such as still existed, for example, in ancient Hebrew teachings. We must learn not always to speak of the contradistinction between matter and spirit. Rather we must see the interplay between what is material and what is spiritual as a unity, especially with regard to our understanding of sense perceptions. As with the Yahweh culture three millennia ago, so this is what nature will become for us, too, when it is no longer regarded as something purely material, or even as something soulful, as it was fantasized to be, for example, by Gustav Theodor Fechner. When we learn to accept in nature what belongs both to the soul and to sense perceptions, then shall we know the relationship of Christ to external nature. Then will the relationship of Christ to external nature come to resemble a kind of spiritual breathing process.

If we increasingly apply a sound common sense to the matter, we shall come to understand that pre-existence is indeed something upon which soul existence is founded. And we must examine our egoistic concept of post-existence, which is egoistic purely because we have the desire to continue existing after death. We must complement this egoistic concept of post-existence with the concept of the soul's pre-existence. Thus we must endeavour in a new way to arrive at a true view of the immortality of the soul. This can be seen as a definition of the Michael culture. If, as we make our way through the world, we are aware that every sight we see, every sound we hear causes something spiritual to stream into us, and if we at the same time allow something of our soul to stream out into the world, then we shall have succeeded in achieving the consciousness needed by humanity for the future.

Let us look again at the image mentioned just now. You see a flame. You shut your eyes and have the after-image which is fading. Is this merely a subjective process? Today's physiologists say it is. But this is not true. In the world-ether it is an objective process just as is the carbon dioxide you exhale into the air. You impress upon the world-ether an image which you experience merely as an image that fades. Rather than being a subjective process it is in fact an objective one. It is objective. If you become aware of it, it gives you the possibility of seeing how something taking place within you is at the same time a subtle process in the world. When I see a flame, and when I let it fade by closing my eyes—of course it also fades when your eyes are open, only then you don't notice it—I am seeing something which is taking place not only within myself but also in the world outside me.

And it is not only in the case of the flame that this is so. When you meet someone and say to yourself: This chap has said something or other which might or might not be true— that is a moral or an intellectual act within yourself. And it fades just as does the flame. It is an objective process. And when you think well of a fellow human being, this fades too; it is an objective process in the world-ether. When you think ill of someone, it fades as an objective process. You cannot confine within your own private closet what you perceive or what you criticize about the world. It may appear to you to be merely a private matter, but in fact it is also an objective process in the world. Just as was the case in the third post-Atlantean age, when breathing was a process within the human being and at the same time an objective process, so must future humanity come to realize that the soul-processes

I have mentioned are at the same time also objective world-processes.

This transformation in consciousness is something which calls for a greater strength to come about in the mood of human souls than that to which we are accustomed nowadays. Becoming filled with this consciousness entails making way for the culture of Michael to enter our souls. If we take light to be the general representative of sense perception, then it is up to us to think of light as being filled with soul, just as was taken for granted by people in the second or the third pre-Christian millennium to think of air. We must thoroughly break our habit of seeing in light what our materialistic age is in the habit of seeing in it. We must thoroughly break our habit of believing that what the sun radiates are merely those vibrations talked about in today's physics or by general human awareness. We must come to realize that it is soul which penetrates the universe on the waves of light. And we must also come to understand that this was not the case in the age preceding our own. What approached us through air in the age preceding our own is what now approaches us through light. Quite objectively there is a difference in the earthly process. Overall, we can speak of there being an air-soul-process and a light-soul-process. [Drawing on the blackboard.]

This is something akin to what we can observe in the evolution of the earth. And midway between the two lies the Mystery of Golgotha signifying the transition from the one to the other. It is insufficient both for the present and for the future of mankind to go on speaking abstractly about what is spiritual, to lapse into some kind of nebulous pantheism or

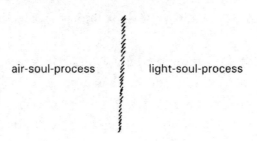

suchlike. What is important is to take what present-day human beings regard as a material process and begin to recognize that it is filled with soul.

We must learn to say: There was a time prior to the Mystery of Golgotha when the earth had an atmosphere, and in that atmosphere there lived the soul which belonged to the soul-element of the human being. Now the earth has an atmosphere which is void of the soul-element which belongs to the human being. Instead, the same soul-element that previously lived in the air has now entered into the light which envelops us from morning till night. This was made possible by the entry of Christ into union with the earth. And thus both air and light have been transformed into something else during the course of earthly evolution.

(30 November 1919)

3. The Soul Lives in the Senses

Human beings are made aware of things in the world[12] through their senses; but their ordinary consciousness does not make them aware of what actually takes place within the senses. If they were aware of this in ordinary life they would be unable to perceive the external world. The senses would, as it were, have to deny themselves if they wanted to make known to human beings what takes place beyond them in the world that lies just outside our earth. If our ears and our eyes were to speak to us we would perceive what was going on in our ears and in our eyes while being unable to hear or see what was externally audible and visible. During the process of learning to know oneself, awareness of the external world must be brought to a halt; one must remain unaware of the external world.

Research in spiritual science has always entailed the endeavour to find methods by means of which the individual can really discover himself. And through my various lectures you will have learned that by self-knowledge I do not mean a generalized brooding about one's everyday self, for that only leads to a kind of reflection of the world around one. It leads to nothing new. It leads only to something that mirrors what one has experienced in the sense-perceptible external world. Genuine self-knowledge, as you know, must seek out methods which silence not only the ordinary, earthly external world but also the ordinary, everyday inward experiences in one's soul which are, when one is properly aware, also merely a mirroring of the external world.

Through the methods described in my book *Knowledge of the Higher Worlds* you know that spiritual research leads initially to what we have termed Imaginative cognition. When we reach such Imaginative cognition, what we initially have before us out of the supersensible world is whatever can be clothed in the images of Imaginative cognition. But once we have gained the ability to see the world through Imagination, the very thing we become able to follow is what can take place within the sense organs of the human being. It is not possible to follow what takes place in the sense organs while perceiving through them anything at all that is happening in the sense-perceptible world.

When I see an object of the external world, my eyes fall silent. Whatever combination of sounds I hear belonging to the external world, my ears fall silent; which means that what one hears through one's ears is not the process taking place within the ears but merely what is entering into them out of the external world. When, for example, our ears are active with regard to the external world, so long as that external perception is present we can never be capable of observing a process taking place inside the ears themselves independently of the external world. As you all know, a sense-impression within the senses continues to work regardless of what the senses are doing so long as we continue to think in a lively way with our normal consciousness.

It is, however, possible for us to abstract ourselves from the whole of the external world, regardless of whether it is a world of colour, a world of sound, a world of smell or whatever, while focusing upon what is taking place in or through our sense organs themselves. If we succeed in this, we arrive at a genuine knowledge about the human being, or rather the first stage of that knowledge. Let us, for example, take the simplest factor into account by trying to understand how an impression made on our eyes by the external world begins to fade. Someone who has attained the gift of Imaginative cognition can, while seeing nothing external, observe this fading of what the senses perceive. The sense organ can be occupied by a process which is taking place in the external world without the person being aware at the same time of that world. With living thinking this can be achieved with all the various senses. Thus we can understand that what actually takes place within the senses can only be observed through Imaginative cognition.

As soon as we live not in the external world but in the senses themselves, a realm of Imaginations is conjured up before our soul. And this shows us that our senses do indeed belong to a world which is different from the earthly world we inhabit. No one who is able by means of Imaginative cognition to observe how his own senses function can ever doubt that although he is a sensory being the human being also belongs to the supersensible world. The realm we come to know through withdrawing from the external world in the manner described is the realm I described in my book *Occult Science* as that of the Angeloi, the world of those beings who are one stage higher than the human being.

What is it that takes place within our senses? We can comprehend it when we observe the inner working of our senses while not actually perceiving anything outwardly. To describe this as a memory would be too inexact. But just as we can have a memory of something we experienced many years ago, even though it is no longer present, so can we indeed gain an insight into our senses by observing the processes which take place in them while they confront the whole world of colours, sounds, fragrances, taste and touch.

It is in this way that we can enter into something of which we otherwise remain permanently unconscious, namely how our senses are active when they are in the process of presenting the external world to us. We thus become aware of how, in the inhalation of air into the human organism and then in its exhalation, the process of breathing works in an extraordinary way throughout our whole organism. When we breathe in, for example, the inhaled air spreads right out into the most delicate ramifications of our senses. And in these most delicate ramifications of the senses the rhythm of breathing meets with that which in spiritual science we term the human being's astral body. What comes about within the senses is founded on the way in which the human being's astral body feels the rhythm of the breath. You hear a sound because the astral body is able to encounter the vibrating air within your organ of hearing. It cannot do this in any other component of the human organism; it is only possible in the senses. In fact, the reason for the existence of the senses is to enable the astral body to come into contact with whatever arises within the human body through the rhythm of breathing. And this occurs not only in the organ of hearing but also in every other sense organ. In every organ of sense, including the sense of touch which is spread out all over our organism, the astral body encounters, in the rhythm of breathing, whatever the air brings about within the organism.

In observing all these phenomena in the human being, we notice that he is not simply an aggregate of solid, physical matter. Thus, for example, his body is also a pillar of almost 90 per cent water. And in a similar way he is also an organism of the air. And this organism of air, a weaving-living entity, meets with the astral body in our organs of sense. This encounter takes place in manifold ways, but all in all we can consider it to be the essential process of perception through the senses. One cannot perceive externally how the astral encounters the air; to do so one must first enter the world of Imagination. Other aspects of our earthly surroundings can also be perceived through Imaginative cognition in the way the astral makes contact with the air. But within us as human beings the essential point is the way in which the astral encounters the processes of breathing.

So in the weaving-living of those beings who belong to the hierarchy of the Angeloi we have to realize that in the unconscious process of perceiving through the senses this world of supersensible beings also weaves and lives in us, coming and going through the gates of our senses. In hearing or seeing we have a process which does not come about within us solely in obedience to our own whim, for it also belongs to the objective world; it takes place in a world which we as human beings do not primarily inhabit, although we are indeed human beings endowed with the senses.

During the period between waking up and falling asleep our astral body is linked, in the realm of our senses, with the rhythm of our breathing and the transformed air which results from this. As a result of this we come to know the outermost periphery of the human being. And it is also possible for us to learn yet more about the human being. This arises at the stage of supersensible knowledge which, in the books mentioned, I have described as Inspired cognition.

Let us envisage how we are subject to the alternation between waking and sleeping. This is not so very different from perception by means of the senses. There is alternation also in the way we perceive through the senses. If we had uninterrupted perceptions we would not interpret them correctly. You are quite familiar with the way in which a sense-impression is impaired if you focus consciously on it for too long. One has to turn consciously away from a sense-impression; one needs to alternate between having the impression and the state of not having the impression. Our awareness with regard to our sense-impressions depends upon our ability constantly to withdraw our senses from the impressions, so that we actually practise sensory perception by means of these brief alternations. And the same comes about over the longer periods of perception through the alternation between waking and sleeping.

As you know, when we enter into the state of sleep our astral body together with our I departs from our physical body and our ether body. So between falling asleep and waking up the astral body becomes connected with the world outside us, whereas between waking up and falling asleep it is connected only with what is going on within the human body. Look at these two conditions or these two happenings. There is the astral body between waking up and falling asleep as it relates to what is taking place within the human physical and ether bodies; and there is the astral body between falling asleep and waking up as it relates to what is going on in the world around us rather than to our physical and ether bodies.

Although this sounds paradoxical, you will understand me when I say that the realm of the senses within us is almost a kind of external world. Consider the human eye, for example. It is like an independent being—of course I am speaking comparatively; it really is like an independent entity placed in a hollow within the skull whence it proceeds to move inwards almost as a matter of course. Looked at separately, however, although it is a living entity it is nevertheless remarkably like an instrument of physics. The processes within the eye are remarkably similar to those which take place in an instrument of physics. Of course the soul embraces these processes, but one can nevertheless describe a sense organ or the realms of the senses, as I have often done, as resembling a gulf or a bay inserted into our own inner being by the external world. The external world extends, as it were, into our senses, and we human beings are far more involved in the external world in our senses than we are in other parts of our organism.

When we observe some organ or other, say a kidney, or any other organ in the human organism, we do not have a sense of participating in anything external by experiencing the processes within it. But when we experience what takes place within our senses we do experience something that is taking place in the outside world. I am not referring to what a physiologist might say about how the senses function. What I mean is a fact which anyone can understand, the fact that a process in the realm of the senses can be experienced as something entering into us from outside, in which we can participate, rather than something which is brought about by our internal organs.

This is also why it is that in our senses the astral body finds itself almost within the external world. Especially when we are participating fully in the external world through our senses, our astral body is virtually immersed in that external world, though this is not the case in the same degree with all the senses. When we are asleep, though, it is indeed fully immersed; so from this point of view one could say that sleep is a kind of intensification of being immersed through the senses in the external world. When your eyes are closed, your astral body withdraws more into your head, it is more your own. When you look thoroughly outwards your astral body enters into your eyes through which it participates in the external world. And when it goes right out of your organism, then you are asleep. To be focused on the external world through the senses is not what we normally imagine it to be, for it is actually a stage along the path towards falling asleep rather than a sign of alert consciousness.

So in perceiving through our senses we human beings participate partially in the world around us, whereas when we are asleep we participate fully in the world around us. And that is when we can perceive with Inspired cognition what is taking place in the world where we find ourselves with our astral body between falling asleep and waking up. And we can also perceive something else with this Inspired cognition, namely the moment when we wake up, when we return. The moment of awakening can be compared with the closing of our eyes, though it is more intense and stronger.

When I have a colour before me I immerse my astral body in that part of my eyes which, as I said, is almost outside of me; I immerse it in the process which is called into being by a colour in the outside world making an impression on my eyes. When I then close my eyes I withdraw my astral body back into myself. And when I wake up from sleep I retrieve my astral body from the external world, from the whole of the cosmos. What I do with the whole of my organism in my astral body when I wake up, I repeat infinitely many times in relation for example to my eyes or my ears while I am awake. The retrieval of the astral body on waking up remains of course unconscious, just as the process of sensory perception remains unconscious. But when someone gifted with Inspired cognition becomes aware of this moment of awakening, he can perceive that this moment of the astral body's re-entry belongs to an entirely different world from the one in which we usually find ourselves. And he frequently also perceives how difficult it is for the astral body to enter once again into the physical and the ether body. It is confronted by hindrances there.

A way of describing this would be to say that when one begins to perceive the process of how the astral body re-enters the physical body, and also the ether body, one experiences spiritual thunder and lightning with all kinds of counter-attacks. These show that the astral body is indeed entering into the physical body and the ether body, but that the physical body and the ether body do not at all resemble what an anatomist or a physiologist would describe. They are, rather, something which belongs also to a spiritual world. What otherwise is the innocent physical body, or what is presumed to be the rather nebulous and innocent ether body, is now revealed as being rooted in a spiritual world. The physical body in its true reality presents itself as something that is quite different from what is perceived by external sense perception, or by ordinary science.

This entry of the astral body into the physical and ether bodies can appear in thousands of different ways; for example it might resemble a burning piece of wood being plunged into water with a thunderous roar. This is merely the simplest or most abstract impression that might appear to one who is only beginning to perceive such things. But the process then becomes inwardly, in manifold ways, more concrete. And gradually it becomes more spiritual so that what appeared initially to resemble roaring thunder and rising turbulence is gradually filled with harmoniously interlacing movements which in all their parts show themselves to be something that can only be described as communicating, as telling something, as presaging something.

At first, however, what is being communicated is clothed in reminiscences of everyday life. But as time passes this is transformed, so that after a while we learn much about a world which also surrounds us and in which we have experiences that cannot be described as experiences coming out of ordinary perception because they are so entirely different in nature, so that we then realize that we are dealing with an utterly different world. So we notice that the human being, on entering with his astral body into his physical and ether bodies, is achieving this with the help of a thorough process of breathing. The astral body, which is at work in the senses, makes contact with the delicate ramifications of the breathing process; it mingles, as it were, with the delicate rhythms in which the breathing process extends into the realm of the senses. On awakening out of the outside world and thus entering into the physical and ether bodies, the astral body takes hold of the whole breathing process which has been left to itself between a person's going to sleep and waking up again. Along the pathways of the breathing process the astral body enters into the physical and ether bodies where it unfurls and spreads out just as the breathing itself spreads out.

When a person wakes up, ordinary consciousness plunges rapidly into perception of the outer world; it quickly combines the experience of breathing with the experience of the overall physical organism. Inspired cognition can distinguish between the way in which the astral body proceeds along the routes of the breathing process while at the same time also perceiving the normal organic processes separately. In fact there is of course no separation between the two. Not only at this moment, but in fact at every moment, the breathing process within the human organism is intimately linked with all the processes in the organism as a whole. But with Inspired cognition a distinction can be made between the two. One can discern how the astral body enters into the physical body along the routes of the breathing rhythm; and in this way one learns about something which otherwise remains entirely unconscious. Having passed through all the objective—not the subjective—states of feeling which accompany this process of entry, one then knows that because the human being is not only a being of the senses but also a being of breathing, he is also rooted in the world which

I termed the world of the Archangeloi in my book *Occult Science*. Just as those beings who stand one stage higher than the human being are active in his senses, so are those spiritual beings who stand two stages above him active in the processes of breathing. They as it were pass into us and out again as we fall asleep and then wake up.

In considering these processes, we find ourselves presented with something that is very significant for human life. If the life we live were to remain uninterrupted by sleep, the impressions we received from the external world would be very short-lived. We would be unable to have permanent memories. You know how quickly the images we receive through our senses fade once they have become after-images. It is true that the images engendered more deeply in our organism last longer. Nevertheless, they too would not survive for longer than a day if we did not sleep.

So what actually takes place during sleep? Let me remind you of something I explained here recently when I described how between falling asleep and waking up the human being experiences in reverse, in his astral body and in his I, whatever he has experienced during the preceding period of wakefulness in the physical world. Let us assume our pattern of sleep and wakefulness is quite regular—although actually the situation is very similar even if it is irregular. Let us assume that we wake up one morning, do whatever we have to do during the day, and then go to bed, where we sleep for a period which is approximately one third of our period of wakefulness. Between waking up and going to sleep this person has had a number of experiences, his daytime experiences. While he is in the state of sleep he then passes backwards through whatever he experienced during the day. Since his life of sleep is more rapid, it takes him only one third of his wakeful time to go backwards through those experiences.

So what has been happening? I am not talking about the body sleeping in accordance with the laws of the external physical world, which of course it does. But if you were to sleep in the conditions which prevail outside the physical and ether bodies in accordance with the same laws that prevail during daytime wakefulness you would be unable to undergo this process, since you would be obliged to go along with time. We are governed by entirely different laws when we are living in our astral body and in our I outside the physical and the ether body, so you would be unable to undergo this process because you would be obliged to go along with time. When we are in our astral body and in our I but outside our physical and ether bodies we are subject to laws which are entirely different.

What, then, happens when this is seen externally? Well, today is the 22nd of December; you woke up this morning on the 22nd of December. This evening you will go to sleep again, and when you once more wake up in the morning your backward journey will have brought you to the morning of the 22nd of December. You will have undergone a process which has taken you backwards. When you wake up on the morning of the 23rd of December, this process will have taken you back to the morning of the 22nd of December. So you wake up. Counter to the laws that your astral body has obeyed between falling asleep and waking up, your astral body now jerks you back into your physical body in the ordinary physical world. Thus, with your I and your astral body you rapidly re-enter your inmost soul-being on the morning of the 23rd of December. You really do undergo this process.

I do beg you to take what I am saying with all due seriousness so that you can grasp it in its full significance. Imagine filling with gas a vessel which has some sort of device by means of which you can compress the gas into a smaller shape so that the body of gas grows ever more dense. This is something that takes place in space. But it can be compared—only compared, naturally—with what I have just been describing. In your astral body and in your I you go backwards to the morning of the 22nd of December and then, on waking up, rush rapidly forwards to the morning of the 23rd of December. You push your soul forwards in time. This is a densification of time, or rather of that which lives within time. This process causes our soul-element, our astral body, to become compressed in time in a way that enables it to retain impressions of the external world not briefly but rather as memories. Just as gas exerts increased pressure when you make it more dense, in other words it gains in strength, so, through this compression of time within you, does your astral body gain the strong power of remembering, the strong power of memory.

We have thus arrived at a conception of something which normally always escapes our notice. We conceive of time as something which moves forward uniformly, with everything occurring in time also moving forward uniformly. As regards space, we know that it is possible to condense what is present there; and its inner ability to expand thus increases. Similarly, although only comparatively speaking, what lives in time can also be condensed, so that its inner strength increases. And in the case of the human being, one of those inner strengths is the power of memory.

And we do, indeed, owe our power of memory to that process which comes about as we sleep. Between falling asleep and waking up again we live in the world of the Archangeloi, and it is together with the beings of the hierarchy of the Archangeloi that we develop the power of our memory. Just as together with the beings of the hierarchy of the Angeloi we develop the power of sense perception and the ability to combine our sense perceptions, so do we develop the more inward, the more central power of memory in the world of the Archangeloi.

There is no true human knowing that is nebulously mystical and arrived at by internal brooding. True human knowing leads us inward step by step and at the same time upward into higher realms. We have been speaking about two such steps today. When regarding the realm of the senses we are in the realm of the Angeloi. And when regarding the realm of memory we are in the realm of the Archangeloi. Self-knowledge is at the same time knowledge of the divine, knowledge of the spirit, because every inward step made by the human being also leads upward into the spiritual world. It may sound paradoxical, but the more profoundly we proceed inwards, the higher do we rise into the world of the spiritual beings. Self-knowledge truly is world-knowledge, namely knowledge about the content of the world, when we take self-knowledge seriously.

Our discussion has also shown us why in ancient times,

when the people of the Orient strove for a more instinctive type of spiritual knowing, the process of breathing was to be made conscious by means of special breathing exercises. One enters a spiritual world as soon as the process of breathing becomes conscious. I need not reiterate that those ancient exercises should not be repeated by today's human beings with their altered constitution. Different exercises, such as the ones described in the books I have mentioned, must replace them. But for both types of knowing—that of ancient, mystical clairvoyance and that of more modern exact clairvoyance—it is valid to say that one can enter into the spiritual world through genuine observation of those processes which take place within the human being.

Nevertheless, there are some individuals who say: But one is delving into something which is not spiritual if one investigates sense-perceptible processes such as breathing processes. In this comparison with a nebulous mysticism these people are describing it as a form of materialistic self-knowledge. Well, do try it! You will soon see that a sense-perceptible process immediately becomes spiritual when one becomes truly familiar with it and that it is merely an illusion to describe it as a material process. And the same goes for the process of breathing. The breathing process is only a material process when observed from the outside. When inwardly observed it is a spiritual process through and through; indeed it takes place in a world far higher than the one we observe through our senses.

(22 December 1922)

4. The Soul Feels in Breathing

There is nothing of human feeling in the mechanism of the nerves.[13] People do not usually reach this conclusion, but it is nevertheless true. So what is involved when human feeling is expressed in the body? How does feeling relate to the body when the connection between a mental image of something on the one hand and the body on the other hand is as I have just described it with regard to the connection of sense perception with the mechanism of the nerves? Spiritual science shows that just as forming a mental image of something is connected with perception and the inner mechanism of the nerves, so is feeling connected in a similar way with the human being's breathing process and whatever this involves. Strange though this may still sound today, the time will come when this will be proved by scientific research; but it can already be definitely stated on the basis of spiritual science. Feeling as it arises initially has nothing to do with the mechanism of the nerves; it is closely linked with the breathing organism. There is however one objection which is relevant here, and that is that surely it is the nerves which put into action everything connected with breathing! I shall return to this when we come to discussing the will. The nerves do not bring about anything which has to do with breathing. It is rather that just as our optic nerves enable us to perceive light and colours, so do we perceive our breathing process itself with the help of our central nervous system, although less clearly. These nerves, usually termed motor nerves with regard to breathing, are nothing other than sensory nerves. They are there, as with the nerves of the brain, so that we can perceive our breathing, although less clearly.

The origin of feeling in its entire spectrum, from strong emotions to gentle feelings, is connected in the body with what takes place in the breathing process and everything connected with it in whatever direction it takes in the human organism. People will in future think quite differently about the bodily characteristics of feeling once they have understood that one cannot simply say that certain streams emanate from some central organ, the brain, and bring about the processes of breathing. It is the opposite which is true. The breathing processes exist, and they are perceived by certain nerves and thus come into connection with them. But the connection is not that feelings originate in the nervous system. And this brings us to a field which has not yet been studied by what is otherwise today's admirable science. The bodily expressions of our feeling life will be wonderfully illuminated when people begin to study the more delicate changes that come about in the breathing process as an accompaniment to one feeling or another.

The process of breathing is entirely different from the process that takes place in the human being's mechanism of nerves. One can, in a certain sense, say of the mechanism of the nerves that it is a true likeness of the human being's life of soul. There is an expression I would like to use which does not yet exist in our language. What I would like to say is that the life of soul paints a picture of itself in the human nervous system; the life of our nerves truly is a painting of our life of soul. Everything we experience in our soul regarding our external perceptions paints itself in pictures into our nervous system. This is what enables us to understand that the life of the nerves, especially in the head, is, even at birth, a true likeness of the life of soul as it emerges from the spiritual world and unites itself with the life of the body.

The objections that arise today, especially from the perspective of brain physiology, regarding the union of the soul, as it descends out of the spiritual world, with the brain, with the organ of the head—these objections will one day be presented as proof of this very connection. Before birth or conception, the soul prepares the wonderful structure of the head from spiritual foundations. During the course of a human life, the head only becomes four times heavier than it is at birth, by comparison with the body, which grows to be 22 times heavier. Thus the head is at birth already thoroughly formed, it is something perfectly complete at birth. Indeed, even before birth it is essentially a picture of the soul's experience because the soul is at work on the head long before any of the physical facts with which we are familiar take place, which then lead to the existence of the human being in the physical world. For the spiritual researcher it is precisely this wonderful structure of the human nervous system, which is an image of the human being's life of soul, that proves not only that the soul descends from the spiritual world but also that forces which exist in the spiritual world lead to the brain becoming a portrait of the life of the soul.

If I now wanted to use an expression to characterize the connection of the life of feeling with the life of breathing similar to the characterization of the connection of the life of nerves with the life of forming mental images, I would describe the life of breathing and everything connected with it as an imprint, a portrait of the life of soul and spirit. So the nervous system is like a genuine picture, an actual portrait, whereas the breathing system can be likened to pictorial writing. The nervous system is a true picture, a real portrait of the soul. And the breathing system is like pictorial writing, like hieroglyphics. In the case of writing in pictures the soul has to make more of an effort, it must already know something in order to interpret what is seen, and this is the case with the life of breathing. The life of breathing is not quite such an exact expression, not quite such a clear picture of the life of soul. It is more like something that can be compared with the relationship between actual pictorial writing and the meaning of pictorial writing. (For a more exact description I would have to refer to Goethe's study of metamorphosis, but we do not have sufficient time for this today.) The life of the soul, then, is more inward in the life of feeling, less bound to the outer processes. That is also why the correlation is missed by more rudimentary physiology. For the spiritual researcher, however, this is precisely what makes it clear that just as the breathing life is connected with the life of feeling, so must this feeling life be freer, more independent within itself, because the breathing life is a less exact expression of the feeling.

So we understand the body more deeply when we consider it to be an expression of what forms the feeling life rather than considering it to be an expression of what forms the life of mental images. However, because the life of feeling is connected with the life of breathing, the spiritual lives in a more lively, a more inward way in the life of feeling than it does in what is merely a matter of mental images, of visualizations which cannot rise to Imagination but is merely a revelation of what can be externally perceived by the senses. The life of feeling is less clear, less obvious, just as pictorial writing gives a less clear representation—I can only speak comparatively—than does an actual picture. But just because of this, what expresses itself in the life of feeling is more deeply within the spiritual than is the ordinary life of mental images. The life of breathing is less of a tool than is the life of the nerves.

(*15 March 1917*)

I said that as things have developed in today's recent culture,[14] an increasingly one-sided view has arisen concerning the relationship between soul and spirit on the one hand and physical, bodily nature on the other. This is expressed in the way the element of spirit and soul is regarded as belonging only to that part of human bodily nature which is present in the nervous system, or specifically in the brain. The soul and spiritual element is assigned exclusively to the brain and the nervous system while the rest of the organism, in relation to the aspect of soul and spirit, is regarded merely as an incidental supplement coming from brain and nervous system—nothing but a kind of adjunct to the brain and the nervous system. I have endeavoured to clarify the results of spiritual research in this matter by pointing out that one can only reach a true view of the relationship between the human soul and the human body by relating the human soul in its entirety to the human body in its entirety.

By doing this we gain a more profound view when we regard the human soul as a whole as being structured into the life of mental images, or thinking, the life of feeling and the life of will. It is only the life of mental images and thinking itself which is bound up with the nervous organism in the manner assumed by current physiological psychology. By contrast, the life of feeling—of course not in the way it is imagined but simply in the way it *arises*—is related to the breathing organism and everything connected with it in the same way as the life of mental images is bound up with the nervous system. We must assign the feeling life of the soul to the breathing organization. And then what we term the life of will must be seen as being related to what we call the metabolism of the physical body, of course right into its most subtle ramifications. And by taking into account the fact that the individual systems intermingle within the organism— metabolism for example also occurs in the nerves—we find that the three systems interpenetrate at the outermost periphery. We can only reach a proper understanding of all this through knowing that just as our will impulses are allocated to processes of metabolism so is our life of forming mental images allocated to the human nervous system, that is to say to the brain.

Initially such things can of course only be regarded as suggestions, and for this reason one objection after another is possible. But I am convinced that when we no longer approach what has just been said on the basis of partial discoveries made by modern scientific research but instead look at the whole spectrum of anatomical, physiological research, then there will be full agreement between what I have stated on the basis of spiritual-scientific research and what is claimed by the natural sciences.

Viewed superficially—if I may cite the following simply as a characteristic example—one objection after another can be found to gainsay such an all-embracing truth. Someone might suggest that we should agree about the fact of certain feelings being linked to the breathing organism, for there can be no doubt that this is true with regard to some feelings. But then someone else might point out how melodies, for example, are perceived consciously and that they are linked to our feeling of aesthetic pleasure. Is it appropriate here to speak of some relationship or other of the organism of breathing with what takes place in the head since it is obviously a physiological experience connected with the organism of the nerves? Well, as soon as one considers the matter properly, the correctness of my assertion becomes entirely clear, for one must consider the fact that with every out-breath an important parallel process takes place in the brain, namely that if it were not prevented by the cranium from rising up it would do just that. And conversely, with an in-breath the brain would sink down somewhat. But since, because of the cranium, it cannot rise or fall, something occurs which is well known to physiology: a change in the bloodstream arises which is known in physiology as *brain-breathing*—certain processes which occur in the surrounding nerves and run parallel with the process of breathing. In this encounter between the process of breathing and what lives in our ears as sound something takes place which points to the fact that in this realm feeling is linked with the breathing process in the same way as the life of mental images is linked with the organism of the nerves.

I wanted to point this out because it is relatively obscure and therefore all the more readily provides grounds for objection. If one could reach an understanding about all the details brought forward by physiological research, one would find that those details do not contradict what was described last time or what has been presented again today.

I shall now continue with our considerations in a manner similar to that begun in the previous lecture. To do this I must look more closely at how the human being develops the life of sense perception in order to show what it means to perceive with the senses, or indeed what the relationship is between sense perception, which leads to the forming of mental images, and the life of feeling and of will—in fact how the human being lives as a being of soul, of body and of spirit.

Through the life of our senses we connect with our sense-perceptible environment. Within our sense-perceptible environment, natural science distinguishes between certain substances, or rather between certain substance types, for it is on these that physical matter depends. If I wanted to discuss this with a physicist, I would have to distinguish between certain types of substance—solid, liquid, aeriform. But as you all know, in addition to these types, natural-scientific research also assumes something else as well. When natural science wants to explain light, it is not satisfied merely to recognize the existence of those substance types I just mentioned; it instead also includes what initially appears to be more subtle than those substance types, namely what one usually refers to as ether. The idea of ether is extraordinarily difficult to grasp. Indeed, the various ideas which have been put forward regarding what ether might be are almost too numerous to mention.

[. . .]

This riddle of the ether,[15] the etheric, can be resolved by practising the inner exercises I have often described and which are discussed in more detail in my book *Knowledge of the Higher Worlds*. When we proceed through these inner soul processes we do indeed gradually reach the etheric from within. The etheric is then immediately present for us. But not until then are we capable of comprehending what sense perception really is, what really occurs in sense perception.

In order to describe this today I must find another angle from which to approach it. Let us look at what actually takes place for the human being in metabolism. In general terms we can regard metabolic processes in the human organism as taking place mainly in the liquid aspect of substance. This can be easily understood by applying even the most accessible scientific ideas on this matter. A metabolic process takes place in the liquid element. A breathing process lives in the aeriform, gaseous element. In breathing we have an interchange between inner and outer processes of air, just as in metabolism there is an interchange between processes of matter which have taken place outside our body and those taking place inside it.

What is it that takes place when we perceive with our senses and then proceed to form mental images? With what is this connected? Just as fluid processes correspond with metabolism and aeriform processes correspond with breathing—what is it that corresponds with perceiving? It is with etheric processes that perception is connected. Just as in metabolism we live in the fluid element, so do we live in the air in breathing, and so do we live in the ether when we perceive. Inner ether processes, inner etheric processes, which take place in our invisible body about which we have just been speaking, meet up in sense perception with external etheric processes. Someone might object by saying that certain perceptions of the senses are obviously metabolic processes, and that this is obvious in, for example, perceptions connected with the lower senses, taste or smell. Well, if we look more closely we notice that although in all such processes, in tasting for example, there is an element involving physical substance, so is there also an etheric process through which we enter into a relationship with the external ether, just as with our physical body we enter into a relationship with the air when we breathe. Without an understanding of the etheric world, an understanding of sense perception and sensation is not possible.

So what actually happens? Well, we can only really know what is happening when we have reached the stage in the inner soul process at which the inner, etheric aspect of the body has become a reality. This will happen when we have attained what I described in recent lectures here as Imaginative cognition. When the exercises, which you can find in the book already mentioned, have given you the strength to see that they are no longer the abstract ideas we normally have but mental images filled with life, these are what we can describe as Imaginations. When these images have become so alive that they are, in fact, Imaginations, then they live directly in the etheric realm, whereas as abstract concepts they live only in the soul; they overlap into the etheric. And when we have progressed so far in inward experimentation that we are able to experience the etheric as a living reality—it is then that we can experience what it is which takes place in sense perception.

Sensation as it arises through sense perception—I can only present this today in the form of results—comes about when the external environment sends the etheric element from the material world into our sense organs, thus creating those gulfs about which I spoke the day before yesterday, so that what is external becomes internal within the sphere of the senses. A sound, for example, exists between the life of the senses and the external world. Then, when the external ether penetrates into our sense organs, that external ether is deadened. But when the external ether, now deadened, enters into our sense organs it is brought back to life through being met by our ether body. Herein lies the essential nature of sense perception. Just as a deadening and an enlivening comes about in the process of breathing when we inhale oxygen and exhale carbon dioxide, so does a process of exchange also take place between the deadened ether and the enlivened ether in sensory experience.

This is an exceedingly important fact that can be discovered through spiritual science. Something which no philosophical speculations can find, something over which the philosophical speculations of past centuries have come to grief countless times—this is something which can only be discovered along the paths of spiritual science. Sense perception can thus be recognized as a subtle process of exchange between the external and the internal ether—as an enlivening by the inner ether body of the ether that has been deadened by the organs of sense perception. Thus, that which comes to us out of our environment, and is deadened by our senses, is inwardly brought to life again by the ether body. And this is what gives us our perception of the external world.

This is extraordinarily important, for it shows us how the human being, when he turns to an experience of sense perception, is alive not only in his physical organism but also in the supersensible etheric and how the entire life of the senses is a living, weaving involvement in the invisible etheric world. This is what, over the centuries, the more insightful researchers have always conjectured but what can only now be elevated to certainty by spiritual science.

(*17 March 1917*)

5. Enlightenment

Enlightenment is the result of very simple processes.[16] Here, too, it is a matter of developing certain feelings and thoughts which slumber in every human being and must be wakened. Only an individual who, with infinite patience, carries out the simple processes strictly and with perseverance can be led to perception of the manifestations of the inner light. One begins by studying different beings of nature in a particular way: for example, a transparent, beautifully formed stone (a crystal), and a plant and an animal. One should endeavour, at first, to direct one's whole attention to a comparison of the stone with the animal in the following way. The thoughts here indicated as examples must pass through the soul accompanied by alert feelings, and no other thought, no other feeling must intrude and disturb the intensely attentive contemplation. The pupil says to himself: 'The stone has a form; the animal, too, has a form. The stone remains *motionless* in its place; the animal changes its place. It is natural impulse (desire) which causes the animal to change its place. Natural impulses are moreover served by the animal's form. Its organs and limbs are in keeping with these impulses. The structure of the stone is not fashioned according to desires but by power that is void of desire.'*

---

* In their bearing on the contemplation of crystals, the facts here mentioned are in many ways distorted by those who have heard of them merely in an outer (exoteric) way, and this has led to practices such as crystal-gazing and the like. These practices are due to misunderstandings. They have been described in many books, but they never form the subject of genuine (esoteric) occult instruction.

If one thinks deeply into such thoughts, while contemplating the stone and the animal with fixed attention, two quite different kinds of feelings will arise in the soul: one kind from the stone, the other from the animal. Initially the attempt will probably not succeed but, little by little, by dint of genuine and patient practice these feelings will ensue. This must be practised over and over again. At first the feelings are present only as long as the contemplation lasts; later on their after-effects continue. And then they become something that remains alive in the soul. The student then only has to reflect and both feelings will always arise, even without contemplation of an external object. Out of these feelings and the thoughts connected with them *organs of clairvoyance* are formed. If the plant is then included in the contemplation, it will be observed that the feeling emanating from it lies midway, both in character and degree, between the feeling which streams from the stone and the feeling which streams from the animal.

The organs thus formed are *eyes of the spirit*. With them the pupil gradually learns to see something like psychic and spiritual colours. The spiritual world, with its lines and figures, remains dark as long as he has achieved only what has been described as Preparation; through Enlightenment it becomes light. Here, too, it must be noted that the words 'dark' and 'light', as well as the other expressions used, describe only approximately what is meant. Nothing more is possible if ordinary language is used, for this language was created for physical conditions only. When a stone is clairvoyantly observed, a colour streams from it which occult science describes as 'blue' or 'bluish-red'; and the emanation from an animal is described as 'red' or 'reddish-yellow'. In reality, the colours seen are of a spiritual kind. The colour emanating from the plant is 'green', passing over into a light, ethereal rose-pink. The plant is a being which in higher worlds resembles, in a certain respect, its make-up in the physical world. This does not apply to the stone or the animal. It must be clearly understood that the above-named colours indicate only the main hues in the stone, plant and animal kingdoms. In reality there are intermediate nuances of every kind. Every stone, every plant, every animal has its own quite definite nuance of colour. There are also the beings of the higher worlds who never incarnate physically; their colours are often wonderful, also often horrible. Indeed, the wealth of colour in these higher worlds is immeasurably greater than in the physical world.

Once a person has acquired the faculty of seeing with spiritual eyes, he encounters, sooner or later, the beings mentioned above, some of them higher than man in rank and some lower; they are beings who never enter physical existence.

If a person has reached the point described here, the ways to a great deal are open to him. But nobody should be advised to proceed still further without paying careful heed to what is said or otherwise communicated by the spiritual investigator. And with regard also to what has already been described, it is always best to pay attention to such experienced guidance. Moreover, if someone has the strength and endurance to reach the point denoting the elementary stages of Enlightenment, he will quite certainly seek and find the right guidance.

Under all circumstances, however, one precautionary measure is necessary, and whoever is unwilling to adopt it would be well advised to abstain from any attempt to make headway in occult science. It is essential that anyone who becomes a pupil should lose none of his qualities as a good, high-minded person or his sensitivity to physical reality. Throughout his training, indeed, he must continually enhance his moral strength, his inner purity and his powers of observation. To take one example only: during the elementary exercises for Enlightenment the pupil must take care to ensure that his compassion for the human and animal worlds and his response to the beauty of nature are constantly increasing. Failing this care, the exercises would continually blunt his feelings and sensitivity; his heart would become hardened and his senses blunted. And that would inevitably lead to dangerous results.

How Enlightenment proceeds when, in line with the meaning of the foregoing exercises, the pupil passes from the stone, the plant and the animal up to man, and how, after Enlightenment, the union of the soul with the spiritual world takes place under all circumstances and leads on to Initiation—of this the following chapters will speak, in so far as this can be done.

In our time the path to occult science is sought by many. It is sought in all sorts of ways, and many dangerous, objectionable practices are tried. It is for this reason that those who claim to know something of the truth in these matters should make it possible for others to learn something about esoteric training. Only as much as conforms with this possibility has been communicated here. It is essential that something of the truth should become known in order to prevent error from causing great harm. No harm can come to anyone who follows the path here described, provided he does not force things. But one thing must be heeded: nobody should spend more time and strength on these exercises than his position in life and his duties allow. Nobody should immediately change anything in the external conditions of his life as the result of taking this path. Without *patience*, no genuine results can be achieved. After a few minutes the pupil must be able to stop the exercises and quietly go about his daily tasks. No thoughts about the exercises should interfere with this. Whoever has not learnt to *wait* in the highest and best sense of the word is not suited to become a pupil of spiritual science and will never achieve results of real value.

Control of Thoughts and Feelings

When someone seeks the paths leading to higher knowledge in the way described in the preceding pages, he should not omit to fortify himself throughout his efforts with *one* continuous thought. He must constantly have in mind that after some time he may have made quite considerable progress without this being apparent to him in the way he may have expected. Whoever forgets this may easily lose perseverance and after a short time give up all attempts. The powers and faculties to be developed are, at the beginning, of a very delicate kind, and differ entirely from any ideas that may have been previously formed about them by the individual concerned. After all, he will have been accustomed to occupy himself with the physical world alone; things of the soul and spirit will have been far from his sight and mind. It is therefore not surprising that when these new powers of spirit and soul are developing within him he may not be immediately aware of them.

Here lies the possibility of error for anyone who sets out on the path to occult knowledge without guidance from the experience gathered by competent investigators. The occultist is aware of the progress made by the pupil long before the latter is conscious of it. He knows how the delicate eyes of spirit are beginning to develop before the pupil has any notion of it. And a large part of what the occultist has to say will be designed to keep the pupil from losing confidence and endurance before he gains his own knowledge of the progress he has made. The occultist, as we know, cannot *give* his pupil anything that does not already lie hidden within him. All he can do is to give guidance for the development of slumbering faculties. But what he communicates from his own experiences will be a support for one who is striving to find his way out of darkness into the light.

Many abandon the path to occult science soon after having set foot upon it because their progress is not immediately apparent to them. And even when the first experiences begin to arise, the pupil often regards them as illusions because he had formed quite different ideas of what they were going to be. He loses courage, either because he considers these first experiences valueless or because they seem to him so insignificant that he does not believe they could lead him to any important results within a measurable time. *Courage* and *self-confidence* are two beacons which must never be extinguished on the path to occult science. No one will ever travel far who cannot bring himself to repeat, over and over again, an exercise that has failed, apparently, for an incalculable number of times.

Long before there is any distinct perception of progress, a dim feeling arises of being on the right path. This feeling should be cherished and fostered, for it can become a trustworthy guide. Above all it is imperative to eradicate the belief that any weird, mysterious practices are required for the attainment of higher knowledge. Let it be clearly realized that the starting point must be the feelings and thoughts of one's everyday life and that these feelings and thoughts need only be given a new, unfamiliar direction. One must say to oneself: 'In my own world of feeling and thought the loftiest Mysteries lie hidden, only I have hitherto not been aware of them.' In the end it all depends on the fact that human beings ordinarily carry their body, soul and spirit about with them but are *conscious* in the true sense only of their body, not of their soul and spirit. The pupil of occult science becomes conscious of the soul and spirit just as ordinary human beings are conscious of their body.

Hence the important thing is to give the thoughts and feelings the right direction, for only then can one develop perception of things that are invisible in everyday life. One of the ways by which this can be done will now be indicated. Again, like almost everything else so far considered, it is a simple matter, but its effects are of the greatest consequence if it is perseveringly carried through in a mood of sufficient sensitivity.

Let the pupil place before him a small seed of a plant. The

point is to intensify the right kind of thoughts while con-templating this insignificant object and through these thoughts to develop certain feelings. First, let him realize clearly what his eyes are actually seeing. Let him describe to himself the shape, colour and all other distinctive features of the seed. Then let him reflect as follows: 'Out of this seed, if planted in the soil, there will grow a plant of complex structure.' Let him visualize this plant, build it up in his imagination and then say to himself: 'What I am now pic-turing in my imagination will later be drawn out of the seed by the forces of the earth and the light. If I had before me an artificial object which imitated the seed to such a deceptive degree that my eyes could not distinguish it from a real seed, no forces of the earth or light could call forth a plant from it.' Whoever lays hold of this thought quite clearly, so that it becomes an experience, will be able to unite the following thought with the *right feeling*. He will say to himself: 'All that will ultimately grow out of the seed is already secretly enfolded within it as the *force* of the whole plant. In the artificial imitation of the seed no such force is present. And yet *to my eyes* both appear alike. The real seed therefore contains something *invisible*, which is not present in the imitation.' It is to this invisible something that thought and feeling are now to be directed.* Let the pupil picture the following to himself: 'This invisible something will after a

---

* Anyone who might object that examination with a microscope would reveal the difference between the real seed and the imitation would only show that he had failed to grasp the point. The aim of the exercise is not to examine the object as seen by the physical senses, but to use it in order to develop forces of soul and spirit.

while transform itself into the visible plant which I shall have before me in shape and colour.' Let him hold firmly to the thought: '*The invisible will become visible.* If I could not *think*, then that which will become visible only later could not already announce its presence to me.'

The following point must be especially emphasized: what is being thought here must also be intensely *felt*. In inner quiet the thought indicated above must be *experienced*, with no disturbing intrusions from other thoughts. And sufficient time must be allowed for the thought and feeling united with it to penetrate the soul. If this is brought about in the right way, then after a while—possibly only after many attempts— an inner force will make itself felt. And this force will create a new power of perception. The seed will appear as if enveloped in a small, luminous cloud. In a sensory-spiritual way it will be felt as a kind of *flame*. The centre of this flame evokes the same impression as that made by the colour *lilac*; the edges give the impression of a *bluish* tint. The plant itself, which will become physically visible only later on, now manifests in a spiritually visible way.

It is understandable that many people will regard all this as illusion. They will say: 'What is the use to me of such visions, such fantasies?' And many will abandon the path. But this is precisely the all-important point: not to confuse fantasy with spiritual reality at these difficult stages of development; and then to have the courage to press forward and not to become timorous and faint-hearted. On the other hand, however, it must be emphasized that the *healthy* reason which distin-guishes truth from illusion must be continually cultivated. During all these exercises the individual must never lose his fully *conscious* self-control. He must practise the same reliable thinking that he applies to the details of everyday life. It would be very bad to lapse into daydreams. Intellectual clarity, not to mention sober common sense, must at every moment be maintained. And it would be the greatest mistake if as the result of such exercises the pupil were to lose his mental balance, if he were drawn away from judging the affairs of his daily life as clearly and soundly as before. He should examine himself again and again to see if his mental equilibrium has been at all disturbed, and whether he has remained *unaltered* in relation to his daily circumstances.

He must preserve an unshakeable inner serenity and a clear mind for everything. Strict care must always be taken not to give oneself up to arbitrary daydreams or to all sorts of different exercises. The directions indicated above have been tested and practised since time immemorial and *no others* are communicated here. Anyone attempting to turn to exercises of a different kind, which he has himself devised or of which he has heard or read somewhere or other, will inevitably go astray and find himself on the path of boundless fantasy.

A further exercise, to be linked on to the one just described, is the following. Let the pupil place before him a fully developed plant. Now let him fill his mind with the thought: 'The time will come when this plant will wither and die. Nothing of what I now see before me will then exist. But the plant will have developed seeds, and these in their turn will grow into new plants.' Once again I become aware that in what I see something I do not see lies hidden. I fill my mind with the thought: 'This plant, with its form and colours, will in time be no more. But the fact that it produces seeds teaches me that it will not vanish into nothingness. At present I cannot see with my eyes what preserves it from disappearance, any more than I could previously see the plant in the seed. *Hence there is something in the plant that my eyes do not see.'* If I let this thought live in me, imbued with the *feeling* that should go with it, then in due time there will again develop in my soul a force which will become *new vision.* Again there will grow out of the plant a kind of spiritual *flame-form*, correspondingly larger, of course, than the one previously described. It may give an impression of blue in the middle and of yellowish-red at the outer edge.

It must be explicitly emphasized that these 'colours' are *not* colours as seen by physical eyes. To apprehend 'blue' *spiritually* means to be aware of or to feel something similar to what is experienced when the physical eye rests on the colour blue. This must be borne in mind by anyone who is intent upon rising gradually to the level of spiritual perceptions. Otherwise he will expect to find in the spiritual a mere repetition of the physical, and that would lead to the most bitter bewilderment.

Whoever has achieved this spiritual sight has gained a great deal, for things reveal themselves not only in their present *state of being* but also in their stages of formation and passing away. Everywhere he begins to see the spirit, hidden from the physical eyes. And thus he has taken the first step towards penetrating with his own vision behind the mystery of *birth and death.* For the outer senses, a being comes into existence at birth and passes away at death. But that is only because these senses do not perceive the hidden spirit of the being. For the spirit, birth and death are merely transformations, just as the sprouting of the flower from the bud is a transformation enacted before our physical eyes. But if we wish to gain direct knowledge of this through our own vision we must first waken the necessary spiritual sense in the way indicated here.

In order to dispose immediately of another objection which might be raised by certain people who have some psychic experience, something more must be said. It is certainly not disputed that there are shorter and simpler paths, and that many people come to know the phenomena of birth and death through their own vision without having first gone through all that has been described here. There are indeed people with considerable psychic gifts, needing only a slight stimulus to bring their gifts to fruition. But they are exceptions. The path described here is safer and more generally suitable. It is possible to acquire some knowledge of chemistry by exceptional methods, but if you wish to become a chemist you must follow the recognized and more reliable course.

It would be a serious mistake for anyone to suppose that he could reach this goal more convincingly if the grain of seed or the plant mentioned above were *merely* pictured, merely visualized in the imagination. This might also lead to the goal, but not as surely as the method indicated here. The vision attained in that way will, in most cases, be only a figment of the imagination, and the transformation of it into genuine spiritual vision will still have to be accomplished. For the point is not that *I* arbitrarily create visions for myself, but that reality creates them *in me*. The truth must well up from the depths of my own soul; but the magician who conjures forth the truth must not be my ordinary ego but the actual beings whose spiritual reality I want to behold.

(*Knowledge of the Higher Worlds*, 1904/1905)

6. Pure Perception

I have told you about the concept of my book[17] *The Philo-sophy of Spiritual Activity.*[*] It is a modest endeavour to reach pure thinking, pure thinking in which our I can live and hold its ground. When one has grasped pure thinking in this way one can then embark on a further endeavour. One can take this thinking, which then feels itself to be living freely and independently within a free spirituality, and detach it from the process of perceiving. Then, whereas in ordinary life we see, for example, a colour by imbuing it in perception, we can detach this from the whole process of perceiving and can bring the whole perception directly into our bodily nature.

Goethe was on his way to achieving this. He had already taken the first steps. If you read the chapters about colour in his *Scientific Studies* you will see how he experiences in every effect something which unites not only with the capacity to perceive but also with the human being in his entirety. He perceives yellow, or red as a colour which is aggressive, piercing right through him and filling him with warmth; or he sees blue and violet as colours, which in a way drag one out of oneself, as cold colours. The human being in his entirety experiences something when he perceives with his senses. The sensory perception together with its content sinks down into the bodily nature while above it the I hovers with its content of pure thought. So we suspend our thinking.

---

*Currently published as *The Philosophy of Freedom*.

Whereas initially we weakened the content of perception through our thinking, we now take the whole content of the perception into ourselves, thus entirely imbuing ourselves with it.

We give ourselves a training in this way of imbuing ourselves with the content of the perception when we practise a symbolic, a pictorial way of conceiving, when we do this systematically, when, instead of absorbing the content of the perception in pure thinking, in logical thinking, we absorb it in symbols, in images. In this way we let it stream into us by circumventing the thinking. Thus, for our schooling, we fill ourselves not through thoughts but through symbols and images with all the fullness of their colours, with all the fullness of their sounds which we experience inwardly. By filling our inner life not with the content of thoughts, after the manner of associative psychology, but rather with a content hinted at through symbols and images, we allow what lives in our ether body and in our astral body to stream towards us from within. And in this way we become familiar with the depths of our consciousness and of our soul. This is truly the way in which we can come to grips with the inner life of the human being, rather than through the waffling mysticism which some nebulous intellectuals tell us is the path to our inner divinity but which actually leads only to an outer abstraction that is entirely unsatisfactory for us if we want to become whole human beings.

If we truly want to examine the human being physiologically, we must suspend thinking and instead enter inwardly into pictorial conception, so that our bodily nature can react in Imaginations. This is, though, a path which is only in its initial stages in occidental development. But it is the path upon which we must set out in order to counteract what is coming over from the Orient, which would lead to decadence if it were to become the only path. We must aim for ascent rather than descent in our civilization. The general situation is that human language itself is not yet capable of giving full expression to the experiences we encounter inwardly in our soul. So I want to recount a personal experience I had.

Many years ago I endeavoured in a specific connection to put into words what one might define as a science of the human senses. To some extent I succeeded by word of mouth in explaining what a science of the human senses might entail, our science of the twelve senses. This was because when speaking one is able, through twisting and turning one's words and through repetition, to counteract the inadequacies of our language which is as yet not up to such super-sensory explanations. But when—as I said, this was many years ago—I wanted to write down as actual anthroposophy what I had presented in lectures, in order to publish it in book form, it turned out that taking something experienced externally into one's inner being is so sensitive that our language lacks the words by which it can be properly described. I seem to remember that the initially printed pages, many of them, lay unfinished at the printer's for five or six years. I was unable to finish writing down what I had begun because the language was simply incapable of expressing what I had thus far reached in my research. Subsequently, overwork has meant that I have to this day been unable to finish that book.

Some people who are less conscientious with regard to

passing on to their fellow human beings what they have learned about the spiritual world might smile at the thought of someone becoming stuck when trying to convey what he has received from the spiritual world. But those who have genuinely experienced the feeling of responsibility regarding the problems of passing on to western humanity what is involved in progressing towards Imagination will know that much effort is needed to find the right words for such a description. It is relatively easy to describe the path of schooling that is involved. This I have done in my book *Knowledge of the Higher Worlds*. But when one wants to explain quite specific results, such as the essence of the human senses as such, when one wants to describe a specific part of the human being's internal organization, then the difficulty arises in how to grasp Imaginations and define them sharply by means of words.

This is, nevertheless, the path which must be trodden by western humanity. Just as eastern individuals felt their mantras to be a way of entering into the spiritual world, so must western individuals learn to progress beyond associative psychology and arrive at the essence of their own being through entering into the world of Imagination. Only by entering into the world of Imagination will they be able to attain true knowledge of humanity. And acquiring this true knowledge of humanity is what must enable humanity to progress.

Because it is up to us to follow a much more conscious path than that followed by eastern humanity, we cannot permit ourselves to say: Well, let's leave it to the future to decide whether natural means will suffice to take humanity into the world of Imagination. No, it is because humanity has reached the stage of conscious development that it is necessary to strive consciously for the world of Imagination; it is wrong to come to a halt at certain stages. What would happen if we were to come to a halt at certain stages? If we did this, we would be unable to meet the ever-increasing scepticism, which is moving from East to West, by counteracting it with what is right. Instead we would be counteracting it with that which results from too deep, too unconscious a union of the spirit and soul with the physical body. The relationship of the spirit and soul with the physical body would become, in a certain sense, too dense.

In fact, apart from thinking too materialistically one can actually *become* a materialist when the spirit and soul unite too strongly with the physical body. In such a case one no longer lives in freedom in the concepts of pure thinking which one has attained. If one imbues one's corporeality with perceptions which have become images, one enters into one's bodily nature with those perceptions. And if one then spreads this around, suffusing humanity with it, then a spiritual phenomenon comes into being with which we are all very familiar, namely dogmatism of all kinds. And dogmatism of all kinds is nothing other than something which, when transferred into the realm of spirit and soul, can become a pathological state, for example agoraphobia and the like; or it can be metamorphosed into a form of fear in all kinds of superstitions. All kinds of dogmatism are liable to arise out of what develops as the unconscious urge for Imagination when it is held back by powerful forces. Such dogmatism must gradually be replaced by that which arises when the world of ideas is brought into the region of the I, when one moves towards Imagination and thereby takes the human being in his true form into one's inner experience, thus passing gradually in a different way, the western way, into the spiritual world. This different way, through Imagination, must become the foundation for the stream of spiritual science which must pass from West to East if humanity is to make progress.

(2 October 1920)

In my book *Knowledge of the Higher Worlds*, a safe path[18] towards spiritual realms is described in a way that can be followed by anyone, but especially by those who have not had any scientific education or training during their life. Today, however, I shall concentrate more on those aspects which are suitable for a scientifically trained person. Experience has shown me—as you will soon understand—that what is described in my book *The Philosophy of Spiritual Activity* explains a path of knowledge which is suitable for those who are more scientifically inclined. *The Philosophy of Spiritual Activity* was not intended to provide what is normally expected of a book these days. Normally a book aims simply to provide information for a reader who will consider the content on the basis of his prior knowledge or his scientific bent. But this was not actually the intention of my book *The Philosophy of Spiritual Activity*. It is therefore not really appreciated by those who simply read a book for the information it contains. It is intended to be something which encourages the reader to use his own thinking activity, a kind of musical score which can only be read with the help of the inner activity of thinking while moving from one thought to the next. The book reckons entirely with the reader's inner activity of thinking. And it also reckons with the transformation which comes about in the soul as a result of that thinking activity.

Someone who does not, after reading this book with the effort of his own soul in thinking, admit to himself that he now finds himself in an element of soul-life which he had thus far not grasped—someone who does not realize that he has in some way moved on from his ordinary thinking into a thinking that is free of the senses, so that in thinking he is free of all bodily conditions, such a person is not reading *The Philosophy of Spiritual Activity* in the right way. He is not reading it in the right way if he cannot admit this to himself. One has to be able to say to oneself: Now, having practised this thinking in my soul, I know what pure thinking is.

It is rather remarkable that the very reality which ought to come about in the soul of someone reading my *Philosophy of Spiritual Activity* is something which remains unrecognized by most western philosophers. Many philosophers have stated that there is no such thing as pure thinking, that all thinking must contain relics, however slender, of a sense-perceptible kind. One cannot but believe that philosophers who make such statements have never truly studied mathematics, or have never properly investigated the difference between analytical mechanics and practical mechanics. Indeed, our bent for specialization has gone so far that people often philosophize without any trace of an understanding of mathematical thinking. Yet it is not, in truth, possible to philosophize without having grasped at least the spirit of mathematical thinking. We have seen the attitude Goethe had towards this spirit of mathematical thinking even though he said that he himself possessed no specific connection with the culture of mathematics. Well, anyway, many deny the very existence of what I hope people will acquire through studying *The Philosophy of Spiritual Activity*.

So let us now assume that someone has worked his way through this *Philosophy of Spiritual Activity* in the manner I have just described while applying his ordinary consciousness to the task. Of course he can then not claim that as a result he has somehow now arrived in the supersensible world. I have purposely written *The Philosophy of Spiritual Activity* in a way that enables it to appear before the world as a purely philosophical work. Just imagine what would have been achieved for anthroposophical spiritual science if I had immediately begun to write spiritual-scientific works. Such works would have been ignored by specialist philosophers who would of course have regarded them as pure dilettantism, as literature for laypersons. Of course I had to begin by writing purely philosophically. I had to present the world with something that was purely philosophical even though it did actually go beyond normal philosophy.

The time had to come when a transition would be made from merely philosophical and scientific writing to spiritual-scientific writing. This took place at a time when I had just been invited to write about Goethe's scientific works as a chapter in a German biography about him. That was during the nineties of the last century. Having written this and delivered it to the publisher, I then immediately wrote my own text about 'Mysticism at the dawn of modern spiritual life and its relationship with present-day culture' in which I described the transition from what was purely philosophical to something oriented more towards anthroposophy. When that was published, my manuscript about Goethe was returned to me (together with the remuneration I was due, so that I would not object). A chapter about Goethe's scientific development written by someone describing mysticism of this kind was evidently no longer required.

Well, so let us now suppose that we have worked through *The Philosophy of Spiritual Activity* with our ordinary consciousness in the way I have described. Having done this, we shall then be in the right frame of mind to strive, in a way that is beneficial for our soul, towards what I described briefly yesterday as the path leading into Imagination. This path that leads into Imagination can be undertaken, in keeping with our western civilization, by endeavouring to focus exclusively on the external world of phenomena and letting it work upon us while excluding thinking, although in such a way that we do nevertheless take it in. As you know, in our ordinary spiritual life, while we are awake we perceive and in perceiving we imbue that which is perceived with ideas; in scientific thinking we interweave what we perceive with ideas, thus systemizing what is perceived, and so on. But having developed the way of thinking which is portrayed by degrees in *The Philosophy of Spiritual Activity* we actually become able to work inwardly in our soul so acutely that by excluding, by suppressing those ideas we become focused entirely on the external perceptions.

Moreover, in order to strengthen the soul forces by

absorbing the perceptions in the right way, without working upon them through ideas, while refraining from appraising them in the normal way by means of ideas, one can instead create symbolic or other images for what one sees with one's eyes or hears with one's ears or experiences through temperature or touch. By in this way causing perceptions to flow, by bringing movement and life into one's perceiving in a manner that does not normally come about through ordinary ideas, but rather through symbolic or artistic perceptions, one more easily becomes able to be imbued by the perception itself.

A good way of preparing for such a way of knowing is also to educate oneself strictly as regards what I have termed phenomenalism, working through the phenomena. At the physical border to knowledge, when one endeavours to interpret atoms and molecules metaphysically not by lazily penetrating the blanket of the senses but by using concepts for ordering the phenomena and following them back to their archetypes, one trains oneself to ignore all concepts in one's approach to the phenomena. And when one in addition also symbolizes the phenomena, when one makes pictures of them, then one acquires a strong force of soul by means of which one can absorb the external world without concepts.

Of course one must not believe that this can be attained over a short period. Spiritual research takes a great deal longer than does work in the laboratory or in the astronomical observatory. And above all it calls for an intensive effort of will: when one has for quite a while practised a method of thinking in symbols in this way, when one has furthermore accustomed oneself to focusing on the images with which one fills one's soul as do the phenomena, which otherwise pass one by in life as one moves from sensation to sensation, or from experience to experience; when one has accustomed oneself to contemplating an image for longer and longer periods, an image which one has made for oneself or been given by someone else so that it can in no way be a reminiscence; when one has accustomed oneself to concentrating again and again on this image—then the inner strength of one's soul is increased so that one finally becomes aware of experiencing within oneself something of which one has previously been totally unaware. When one lives through such images, this is something totally real and one comes to realize that one is meeting within one's inner being the spiritual element which gives rise to the process of growth, which indeed actually is the process of growth. One notices, one enters into a part of one's human make-up which is within one, which unites itself with one, which is active within one but which until now one has experienced only unconsciously. In what way has one experienced it unconsciously?

Well, I have explained to you that from birth until the change of teeth there is an element of spirit and soul which organizes the human being from within but which then gradually emancipates itself. Then, between the change of teeth and sexual maturity there is an element of spirit and soul which enters into the physical body, initially stimulating the love-urge, but subsequently also much else. All this occurs unconsciously. But if one comes to experience such processes in full consciousness, with the ability to follow the entry of spirit and soul processes into the physical body, then one sees, in the way such processes take place within the body, that the human being is already given over to the external world from birth onwards. Such being-given-over to the external world is today considered to be a merely abstract observation. But it is not.

We are surrounded by a world of colour, a world of sound, a world of warmth and so on. And all this makes an impression on our senses, which we work through in the realm of ideas that in turn again bring new impressions to our organism. When we experience consciously all these things which we have been experiencing unconsciously since our childhood, when we absorb all those impressions of colour and all those impressions of sound, we find that something spiritual is imbuing our organism. So when, for example between the change of teeth and sexual maturity, we take in the sensation of love, this is not something arising out of our body; it is something given to us by the cosmos through the colours, the sounds, the sensations of warmth which approach us from out of the cosmos. Warmth is something other than warmth in the physical sense, light is something other than physical light, sound is something other than physical sound. When we experience sense-impressions, we do of course initially notice the external sound or the external colour. But what works through these impressions is not what modern physics or modern physiology might surmise to be etheric movements, or movements of atoms and suchlike. What is at work in them is spirit, the forces of spirit which make us what we are as human beings in the physical world between birth and death.

And when we embark on paths of knowledge such as those

I have described we discover how we have been organized from out of the external world. We are able to observe consciously what is at work within us because we now have a clear realization that spirit is at work in the external world. Through the phenomenology we arrive at the ability to see clearly how spirit is present in the external world. Not through abstract metaphysics but through phenomenology we reach our knowledge of the spirit. Through our heightened awareness we perceive what we otherwise do unconsciously; we perceive how the spirit enters into us and organizes us from within ourselves.

As I told you yesterday, the oriental wise man does not, in a way, take into account the significance of what is spoken, the significance of what is thought, the significance of how the I is perceived; he has a different feeling, a different attitude of soul towards these things because speaking, perceiving thoughts, perceiving the I initially distract us from the spiritual world and instead cause us to relate socially to our fellow human beings. In ordinary physical life we, in a way, gain our existence in our social environment through making speaking audible, through making thinking transparent and through making it possible for perception of the I to take place through feeling. The oriental wise man, on the other hand, accepted the inaudibility of the word and thus lived in the word. He accepted the non-transparency of the thought and thus lived in the thought, and so on. We here in the West are to a greater degree dependent on having to look back towards the human being on our way into spiritual worlds.

Let us remember that the human being has a certain organization of the senses also in his inner nature. I have already explained how we have three senses within us through which we perceive ourselves inwardly in the same way as we perceive the world outside ourselves. We have a sense of balance through which we feel ourselves appropriately in the space around us and are thus able to work there with our will. We have a sense of movement through which we are able to feel inwardly that we are moving, even if we are in the dark. And we have a sense of life through which we are able to feel our overall state of being as it varies in varying life situations. These three inner senses collaborate with our will, especially during the first seven years of our life. In accordance with our sense of balance we are transformed from a being who can only crawl into one who can stand up and walk. This is brought about by our sense of balance as it places us in the world through our upright gait. And in a similar way we are brought into our full humanity by our sense of movement and our sense of life.

Someone who is able to observe, as objectively as one does in a laboratory, how the human being develops his spirit and soul, and also his physical nature, will see how that which organized him through and through primarily during the first seven years of his life then emancipates itself, assuming a somewhat different guise after the period of the change of teeth. The human being is then no longer so intensively bound up with his inner being as he was as a small child. The small child is intensively bound up with human balance, with human movement and with human life.

But then, while this emancipation of balance, movement and life is proceeding, something else is also beginning to happen. In a certain way three other senses, the sense of smell, the sense of taste and the sense of touch develop. Although it is more obvious earlier on, someone schooled in such observation can continue to observe this later. It is most interesting to watch how the child gradually finds his way into life in orientation through the sense of smell, the sense of taste and the sense of touch. He as it were pushes out of himself the senses of balance, movement and life, and he thus in a way draws into himself all the qualities that belong to the sense of smell, the sense of taste and the sense of touch. One could say that over a longer period of life the one aspect is exhaled while the other is inhaled, so that within our organism, as they move outwards, the forces of balance, movement and life encounter the inward-pushing forces of smell, taste and touch. The one trio of senses intermingles with the other trio of senses. What comes about through this intermingling is a firm self-consciousness; it is through this that the individual feels that he has become a proper self.

Just as we are closed off by external spirituality—quite rightly, since we would otherwise not become social beings in physical life—just as we are closed off by external spirituality through speech, through perception of thoughts and through perception from the I of another individual, so, because the qualities of smell, taste and touch grow towards balance, movement and life, are we cut off inwardly from this trio of life, movement and balance which would otherwise be directly perceptible to us. Experiences of the sense of smell, of the sense of taste and of the sense of touch intervene between us and what we would experience as the sense of balance, the sense of movement and the sense of life.

The oriental wise man comes to a halt in speech in order to

live within it, comes to a halt in thinking in order to live within it, and comes to a halt in perception of the I in order to penetrate outwards into the spiritual world. In the same way, with us, as we develop towards Imagination, we imbibe external perception without perceiving it, thus carrying out the opposite activity from what the oriental wise man does with regard to speech, thinking and perception of the I. He comes to a halt here. He lives his way into these activities. Someone striving for Imagination, however, twists his way through the perception of smell, taste and touch as he penetrates inward, so that by remaining unobstructed by the perception of smell, by the perception of touch and by the perception of taste he approaches what can be experienced through balance, movement and life.

It is a great moment when one penetrates through all that I have described as the trio of the senses of taste, smell and touch and is then starkly confronted with what exists in movement, balance and life.

Having been prepared in this way, it is interesting to examine what is so often presented by western mysticism. I am of course far from wanting to underestimate all that is poetic or beautiful or imaginative in numerous kinds of mysticism. Of course I admire what has been given to us by Saint Teresa, or by Mechthild of Magdeburg and others, for example even by Meister Eckhart and Johannes Tauler. But for a true researcher of the spirit all this is revealed when one follows the inward path without passing through the region of smell, of taste or touch. Read what has been written by some individuals who have described in detail what they have experienced in this respect. They describe a kind of tasting of their inner life, a tasting of the element of spirit and soul in the inner human being; they also describe a kind of smelling, and even a kind of touching in a certain sense. Someone who understands these things will see quite clearly in what is said by individuals like Mechthild of Magdeburg or Saint Teresa that although they are following this inward path they are unable to pass beyond smelling, tasting or touching. They describe their experiences in beautiful, poetic images, but what they are describing is only how they are smelling their inner being, how they are tasting their inner being or how they are touching their inner being.

Indeed, to perceive the true character of reality with properly developed spiritual sight is not as enjoyable as finding it being described by a voluptuous mysticism—for voluptuous is in fact what it is—which actually only satisfies a kind of refined, inward-looking egoism of soul. Much though I marvel at and admire this kind of mysticism, I cannot but point out that for a genuine spiritual researcher this mysticism only goes halfway. What is shown by the beautiful and poetic images described by Mechthild of Magdeburg or Saint Teresa is in reality nothing other than what one attains through smell, taste and touch prior to entering fully into one's inner being.

Truth is occasionally unpleasant, perhaps sometimes even cruel. But it does not behove present-day humanity to become rachitic in soul through pursuing a nebulous, imperfect mysticism. What behoves our present time is to enter fully into our inner being with spiritual strength, with that strength which we apply, with no little success, in a far more disciplined way to the natural sciences. The natural sciences are accepted for the very reason that they are disciplined and methodical. And through the very fact of having worked scientifically, we know that even though we can fully appreciate what comes from a nebulous mysticism such nebulous mysticism is nevertheless not what must be practised nowadays by a spiritual science. What spiritual science is required to do is search for a clear understanding of one's own being so that from this a clear spiritual understanding of the external world can emerge.

If I were to refrain from saying these things, which I know I must say for the sake of the truth, I would no doubt gather a following of all those nebulous mystics who practise mysticism for the sake of attaining an inner voluptuousness of soul. But this cannot be done in connection with what we want to practise here; our task is to find the strength for life, the strength which, as a strength of spirit, can be brought into our scientific and our social life.

When we have progressed to the stage of finding what lives in the sense of balance, in the sense of life and in the sense of movement, we will have reached something which, on account of its clarity, we initially experience as the true inner nature of the human being. From the very nature of the matter, we know that we can go no deeper. And initially this does indeed suffice. For that of which the nebulous mystics dream is not what we have found. What we find is a genuine spiritual organology, the true being of that which is infused with balance, with movement and with life. This is what we find within our inner being.

And when we have done this something remarkable has occurred. One notices something at this moment. I have taken for granted that we have thoughtfully studied *The Philosophy of Spiritual Activity*. And, having then put it on one side, we have set out to follow the path of contemplation, of meditation, towards our inner being. We have progressed as far as balance, as far as movement, and as far as life. We live in this life, in this balance and in this movement. And now, although we have done nothing other than follow this contemplative, this meditative path, something arises side by side with our thought-filled work regarding *The Philosophy of Spiritual Activity*. Through our work in pure thought with this philosophy of spiritual activity, through working in our soul in quite a different realm, we have now reached something entirely new. Our thinking has grown more whole, more filled with content.

By going right into our inner being and deepening Imagination, we have raised beyond our ordinary consciousness what we gained through working in thinking with *The Philosophy of Spiritual Activity*. Out of ordinary thoughts, which initially lived in a relatively abstract way in the realm of thinking, we have created forces filled with content that now live in our consciousness. What were formerly pure thoughts have become Inspiration. We have further cultivated Imagination, and pure thinking has become Inspiration. Continuing along this path—or rather two quite distinct paths— we reach the stage of being able to distinguish between on the one hand the life, which at a lower stage is thinking and at a higher stage is Inspiration, and on the other hand what we experience as the state of balance, the state of movement and the state of life. And now we can combine these two types of experience with one another. We can combine what is external with what is internal. And through the combination of Inspiration and Imagination we arrive at Intuition.

What, then, have we accomplished? Let me describe this from yet another angle. To do this I must first point out how the oriental wise man progresses. Having worked with mantras, thus living in language, in words, he then moves on beyond the rhythms of language in order to experience the process of breathing, rather artificially, by varying his breathing in all kinds of ways. For him this represents the next step up, which again cannot be directly applied in our western culture. What does the oriental yoga pupil achieve by consciously regulating his breathing in many different ways? Well, as he breathes in he experiences something very remarkable. As he breathes in he experiences what is present in the air, not only what is physically present, but also what is there when we unite it with ourselves and thus comprehend it spiritually. Through taking in a breath, someone who is a genuine yoga pupil has an experience of what organizes him inwardly, what organizes him spiritually, which in this life does not end with death; he experiences how through the spirituality of the external air something is created within us which continues on beyond the portal of death.

To experience consciously the process of inhalation means to experience within oneself that which remains permanent even when the body is laid aside. To experience consciously the process of breathing, to experience consciously the inward reaction to inhalation, means to experience that which in our spiritual and soul existence prior to our birth, or indeed prior to conception, was already at work in the shaping of our embryo and which then continued to work within us throughout our childhood. To experience consciously the breathing process means to comprehend oneself on the far side of birth and death. To proceed beyond the experience of speech, of the word, in order to experience the breathing process means entering even further into an Inspired comprehension of the eternal in the human being. We westerners have to experience this in a different sphere.

Actually, what is the process of perception? It is nothing other than a modified process of inhalation. As we inhale the air, this air presses down on to our diaphragm, onto the whole of our organism. Cerebrospinal fluid is pushed upwards towards the brain through the spinal cord. In this way a connection is established between brain activity and in-breathing. And that aspect of the inhalation process which becomes specialized in this way in the brain—that is what works through the senses as perception. So, one could say that perception is an offshoot of inhalation. And when we look at exhalation—the cerebrospinal fluid presses downwards, onto the circulation of the blood. The descent of the cerebrospinal fluid is linked to will activity, which is thus linked to exhalation.

Now, a person who has really studied *The Philosophy of Spiritual Activity* will find that in the thinking activity which leads to pure thinking will and thinking coincide. Pure thinking is, basically, an expression of will. Thus pure thinking is related to that which the oriental wise man experienced in the process of breathing out. Pure thinking is related to exhalation in the same way as perception is related to inhalation. For us, it is necessary that we practise the same process as that followed by the oriental student with his yoga philosophy, only it must be pushed further back into our inner being. Yoga philosophy counts on a regular in-breathing and out-breathing in order to reach what is eternal in the human being. And what can the westerner do? He can distinguish clearly in his soul between perception on the one hand and thinking on the other hand. He can take what is normally seen as perceiving and thinking in the abstract and unite them inwardly, so that he experiences inwardly in spirit and soul what is physically experienced as breathing in and breathing out. Physically one experiences breathing in and breathing out; and in their combination one then has a conscious experience of the eternal. Ordinary experience gives us perceiving and it gives us thinking. But through bringing movement into our life of soul we experience the pendulum swing, the rhythm, the never-ending co-vibration of perceiving and thinking.

For the oriental student, a higher reality comes about through inhalation and exhalation. The western student, on the other hand, develops within himself a living process of modified inhalation in perception and a living process of modified exhalation in pure thinking by interweaving think-ing and perceiving; in this way he develops the breathing in spirit and soul rather than the physical breathing of yoga philosophy. In this way, through this rhythmical pendulum swing, through this rhythmical attainment, in breathing, in perception and in thought, he gradually battles his way up to the genuine spiritual reality of Imagination and Inspiration and Intuition.

I may initially have been suggesting only philosophically in my *Philosophy of Spiritual Activity* that true reality is reached through the interweaving of perception and thinking. But this *Philosophy of Spiritual Activity* was actually intended to demonstrate an inner cultivation of the soul which we in the West can practise so that we may ourselves enter into the spiritual world. The oriental scholar says: systole, diastole; breathing in and breathing out. We in the West must say instead: perceiving, thinking. The eastern scholar says: train physical breathing. The westerner says: in order to gain knowledge, train the breathing of spirit and soul through perceiving and thinking.

(3 October 1920)

7. Intensifying Perception

A second aspect that can be developed by the seeker[19] in his inner life of soul comes about when, instead of meandering on and on in thoughts arising from the external world, he surrenders himself to his memories. An entirely different experience results when we abandon ourselves to our memories in a profoundly inward way. The experience of thinking I described just now leads one to oneself; one begins to comprehend oneself, and this is a rather satisfying experience. On the other hand, moving towards an experience of memories does not, if one goes about it in a properly inward way, lead to an experience of oneself. Through thinking one arrives at a freedom which results entirely from what is personal. That is why a philosophy of freedom must arise out of an experience of thinking, for an experience of thinking leads the individual to himself, so that he discovers himself to be a free personality.

This is not the case when we experience memory. When we experience memory, if we take it utterly seriously, entering into it totally, a feeling of becoming detached from oneself, of escaping from oneself, arises. That is why memories, which allow us to forget the present moment, are the most satisfying of all. They may not necessarily be the best, but in many cases they are the most satisfying.

We come to understand fully the value of remembering when we are able to have memories that also carry us out into the world even if we are thoroughly dissatisfied with the present time and would rather escape from it. If we can develop memories that enhance our feeling of being alive through abandoning ourselves to remembering, we gain a sense of preparing ourselves for what memories can become as they grow ever more real.

Memory can become ever more real when you recall as vividly as possible something you experienced years, or even decades ago. Perhaps you could turn to your old possessions and seek out, say, some letters you wrote dealing with a specific event. You lay these letters out in front of you and try to live your way into that past event. Or better still, rather than taking letters you yourself wrote or indeed received from someone else, which can be too subjective, you could find your old exercise books from your schooldays and look at them as you did when you were actually a pupil at school. In other words, turn to something which actually did happen to you during the course of your life. This can be quite remarkable, for it changes your whole mood of soul now in the present time. All you need is to be a little bit inventive. Anything will do. A lady might find an old dress or something she wore 20 years ago; she puts it on and is thus transported into the situation when she last wore it. Just find something that transports your past as vividly as possible into the present. In this way you can separate yourself strongly from your experience of the present as it is now.

When you experience something with your ordinary consciousness, the experience is too close. You need to stand apart from yourself. For example you are more distant from yourself when you are asleep than when you are awake. When you are asleep you are outside your physical body and your ether body with your I and your astral body. You come closer to your astral body, which is outside your physical body when you are asleep, when you call up past experiences as vividly as possible. You will not believe this at first because you will not believe, for example, that something as insignificant as putting on an old dress can have such a strong effect. But it is really important to try such things out. And when you do try them out, when you conjure up an old experience and live in it now, you will see how close you come to your astral body, your sleeping astral body.

However, if you expect that all you have to do is look to one side or the other in order to see your astral body as a nebulous form beside you, you are mistaken. That is not what happens. You must pay attention to what really does happen. What really does happen in such a situation is, for example, that after a while you begin to see the red sky of the morning as something entirely different from what you previously experienced; your experience of a sunrise is entirely different. Gradually in this way you will begin to sense that the warmth of the morning's red sky has something prophetic in it, a naturally prophetic force. You will begin to feel that the blush of the dawn is something spiritually powerful and, though you might at first think it is an illusion, you will detect an inner significance in this prophetic force, namely that the red of the sky at dawn is something in which your very being is bound up.

Experiences of this kind will enable you to look at the red sky in the morning and say: Yes, this red sky does not isolate me. It is not merely over there while I am over here. I am intimately bound up with this redness of the dawn. It is my own inner disposition; I myself am at this moment a red dawn sky. When you have merged in such a way with the redness of morning that it is you yourself who radiates this shining colour, and when you yourself are experiencing how the sun emerges out of that shining colour, so that you live in the feeling of a shining morning sun emerging in your heart, then you gain a sense of moving across the sky's dome together with the sun, a sense that the sun does not desert you, that it is not the sun over there while you are over here, but that your own existence extends right up to the sun's existence and that with its light you are moving through the day.

When you develop this feeling—which, as I have said, does not arise out of thinking, for that is what brings you closer to yourself—when you develop this feeling, these experiences, through remembering in the way I have described, then it is out of this remembering, or rather out of the power of this remembering, that things which you formerly perceived with your physical senses begin to develop a new aspect: these things become transparent for your spirit and soul. Even when you have only once gained a feeling of moving with the sun, when you have won the strength to move with the sun, then you will have a different view of all the flowers in the field. The flowers do not merely continue to show you the yellow or red colours on their surface, for now they begin to speak spiritually to one's soul. The flower becomes transparent. A spiritual essence of the plant rises up in your inner being, and its flowering comes to resemble speaking. This is the way in which we unite our soul also with external nature. We gain in this way an impression that there is something else behind nature's existence, namely that the light, with which we have united ourselves, is sustained by spiritual beings. And in these spiritual beings we gradually then come to recognize characteristics of what is described in anthroposophy.

[...]

One might now be tempted to believe that this simply proceeds ever further and further,[20] that one progresses ever further away from thinking, from the experience of thinking towards the experience of remembering. But this is not the case; things are different. If you really develop within you this experience of thinking, you will in the end gain an impression of the third hierarchy: Angeloi, Archangeloi, Archai. Just as you can imagine how food is processed in your digestion and so on as a bodily experience in gravity here on the earth, so can you imagine the conditions in which the beings of the

Experience of thinking: Third Hierarchy

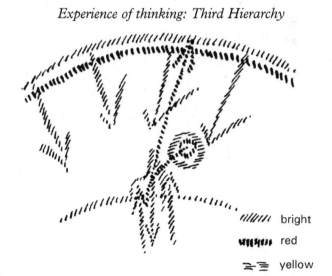

/////// bright

ΨΙΙΨΙΙΙ red

⋑⁼⋑ yellow

third hierarchy live when, through the experience of thinking, you feel how, rather than going about here on the earth, you are instead being borne up by forces which come to you from the ends of the earth.

However, when you move on from the experience of thinking to the experience of remembering, your experience does not—let's say this is the end of the worldly sphere— proceed all the way up to it. When you enter into the reality of the thinking experience, you can reach a world-end of this kind; but then you do not proceed outwards even further. What happens then is that you have here an object, let's say a crystal, a flower, an animal. If you then move on from the experience of thinking to what the experience of remembering can bring, then you look right into this object.

When you have reached the widths of worlds, what you then find through the experience of remembering is that you can look right into things. In other words, you do not penetrate ever further outwards but instead you look inwards into things; you see what is spiritual in all things. For example, in light you see the spiritual beings who are at work in the light; in the dark you see the spiritual beings who are at work in the dark. Thus we can say: The experience of remembering leads into the second hierarchy.

Experience of remembering: Second Hierarchy

(*23 November 1923*)

8. Purifying the Life of Thought and of Feeling

When an individual develops his feelings, thoughts and attitudes in the way described in the chapters dealing with the stages of Preparation, Enlightenment and Initiation, he brings about in his soul and spirit an organic membering similar to that brought about by nature in his physical body.[21] Before this development, soul and spirit are undifferentiated masses. The clairvoyant perceives them as interlacing, cloudlike spirals, dully gleaming with reddish, reddish-brown or even reddish-yellow tints; after development they begin to assume brilliant yellowish-green or greenish-blue colours and display regularity in their structure. This regularity, which leads to higher knowledge, is achieved when the pupil brings into his thoughts, feelings and attitudes a harmony such as that with which nature has endowed his bodily functions, enabling him to see, hear, digest, breathe, speak and so on. The pupil learns gradually to breathe and see with the soul, to speak and hear with the spirit.

Some further *practical* aspects of the higher education of soul and spirit will be treated here in greater detail. They are of such a kind that anyone can give effect to them without taking account of other rules, and thereby be led some way into occult science.

A particular effort must be made to cultivate the quality of *patience*. Every impulse of impatience has a paralysing, even a destructive effect upon the higher faculties that slumber in the human being. Boundless insights into the higher worlds must not be expected from one day to the next, for then as a rule they will certainly not come. Contentment with the smallest achievements, calmness and composure must more and more take root in the soul. It is quite understandable that the pupil will await results with impatience; but he will achieve nothing as long as he fails to master this impatience. Neither is it of any use to combat this impatience merely in the ordinary sense of the word, for then it only becomes so much the stronger. We then deceive ourselves about it and it takes root all the more firmly in the depths of the soul. It is only when we surrender ourselves again and again to a very definite thought, adopting it with every fibre of our being, that any result can be achieved. This thought is as follows: 'I must do everything I can to further the development of my soul and spirit; but I will *wait quite calmly* until higher powers have found me worthy of definite Enlightenment.'

When this thought becomes so powerful in the pupil that it grows into an actual trait of his character, he is treading the right path. This trait will then be evident even in his outer appearance. His gaze becomes steady, his movements become more purposeful, his resolution decisive, and everything that goes by the name of nervous tension gradually disappears. Rules that seem trifling and insignificant must be taken into account. For example, suppose someone affronts us. Before training, our feeling would have been roused and directed against the offender; anger would have surged up from within us. In such a case, however, the thought that immediately arises in the mind of the pupil is: 'This insult does nothing to change my true value.' And then he does whatever has to be done to counter the insult with calmness and composure, not in anger. Naturally it is not a matter of passively accepting every insult, but of acting with the same calmness and assurance when countering an insult against our own person as we should if the insult had been directed against someone else on whose behalf we had the right to intervene. It must always be remembered that occult training is not carried out through crude, external processes, but through delicate, silent transformations in the life of feeling and thought.

Patience attracts the treasures of higher knowledge; impatience repels them. In the higher regions of existence nothing can be achieved by haste and unrest. Above all things, *desire* and *craving* must be silenced, for these are qualities of the soul from which all higher knowledge shies away. Valuable as all higher knowledge is, we must not crave for it if it is to come to us. He who wishes to have higher knowledge for his own sake will never attain it. And this requires above all that in the deepest depths of the soul a person shall be *honest* with himself. He must be under no illusion whatever concerning his own self. With inner truthfulness he must look fairly and squarely at his own faults, weaknesses and inadequacies. As soon as you try to excuse to yourself any one of your weaknesses, you have laid a stone in the path that is to lead you upwards. You can remove such obstacles only by becoming clear about yourself. The *only* way to get rid of faults and failings is by recognizing them for what they are. Every faculty is slumbering in the human soul and can be awakened. An individual can also improve his intellect and reason if he quietly and calmly brings home to himself why he is weak in this respect. Such self-knowledge is naturally difficult, for the temptation to be deluded about one's own nature is immeasurably great. Whoever makes a habit of being truthful with himself opens the portals to higher insight.

Every kind of curiosity must be removed from the pupil. He must rid himself as far as possible of the habit of asking questions about matters on which he wants information merely for the sake of satisfying his personal curiosity. He should ask only about matters which can help to make his own being a more effective servant of evolution. Nevertheless his delight in knowledge and his dedication to it should in no way be weakened. He should listen attentively to everything that serves this aim and seek every opportunity for practising this reverence.

Education of the life of *wishes* is especially necessary in the process of occult development. This does not mean that we should have no wishes. We must wish for anything that we are to attain, and a wish will always tend to be fulfilled if backed by a particular force. This force is derived from right *knowledge*. 'Do not wish at all before you have recognized what is right in any particular domain.' That is one of the golden rules for the pupil. The wise man first learns to know the laws of the world and then his wishes become powers which prove their efficacy. The following example will bring this out. Many people wish to learn from their own vision something about their life before birth. Such a wish is altogether useless and leads to no result as long as the individual in question has not acquired, through study of spiritual science, knowledge of the laws of the nature of the Eternal, in their subtlest, most intimate character. But if he has really acquired this knowledge and now wants to make further progress, *then* his wish, ennobled and purified, will enable him to do so.

It is also useless to say: 'I want to survey my preceding life and to learn with that purpose in view.' We must far rather be able to abandon and eliminate this wish altogether and to learn, at the outset, with no such intention. For only in this way do we learn how to foster the corresponding wish in such a way that it brings fulfilment in its wake.

★

If I get *angry* or *annoyed*, I build a wall around myself in the soul-world, and the forces which should develop my eyes of soul cannot approach. If, for example, a person annoys me, a psychic current goes out from him into the soul-world. I cannot see this current as long as I am myself still capable of anger. My own anger conceals it from me. I must not, however, believe that when I no longer get angry I shall immediately have a psychic (astral) vision of the phenomenon. For this purpose an eye of the soul must first develop in me. The rudiments of such an organ are present in every human being. It remains ineffective as long as he is capable of anger. But neither is it immediately present when anger has been combated to a small extent. We must rather persevere in this combating of anger and patiently continue to do so; then one day we shall be aware that this eye of soul has opened.

Anger is certainly not the only failing to be combated in order to attain this end. Many become impatient or sceptical because they have fought against certain traits of soul for years, and yet clairvoyance has not developed. They will have cultivated certain qualities while allowing others to run riot. The gift of clairvoyance first manifests when all the qualities that hinder the emergence of the slumbering faculties are suppressed. Certainly the beginnings of vision (or of hearing) are present at an earlier stage; but these frail shoots are readily subject to errors of every kind and, moreover, they easily die if they are not carefully tended.

Other traits which have to be combated as well as anger and irritability are timidity, superstition, prejudice, vanity and ambition, curiosity, eagerness to impart unnecessary information and the tendency to make distinctions among human beings according to the outer characteristics of rank, gender, race, and so forth. In our time it will be extremely difficult for people to grasp that the combating of such traits has anything to do with enhancing the faculty of cognition. But every spiritual scientist knows that much more depends upon such things than upon the growth of intelligence and the practice of contrived exercises. Misunderstanding can very easily arise if people believe that they should be foolhardy because they ought to be fearless, or that they should be blind to the differences in human beings on account of having to fight against prejudices connected with rank, race and so forth. The fact is rather that we come to see things truly only when we are no longer steeped in prejudice. Even in a quite ordinary sense it is true that fear of some phenomenon will prevent me from judging it rightly, that racial prejudice will prevent me from seeing into a man's soul. It is this ordinary attitude that the pupil must develop further, with great delicacy and precision.

Every word spoken without having been thoroughly clarified in thought is a stone thrown in the way of esoteric training. And here something must be taken into consideration which can be explained only by an example. When something is said to me to which I have to reply, 'I must try hard to pay more heed to the speaker's opinion, feeling and even his prejudice than to what I myself have to say at the moment about the matter in question'—here is indicated a delicate quality of tact, to the cultivation of which the pupil must dedicate himself. He must learn to judge what importance it may have for the other person if he opposes the latter's opinion with his own. This does not mean that he should withhold his opinion. There is no question whatever of that. But he must listen to the other person with the closest possible attention and form his own reply out of what he has heard. In a case of this kind a particular thought occurs again and again to the pupil and he is treading the right path if this thought lives within him so strongly as to become a feature of his very character. This is the thought: 'The important point is not that my opinion differs from that of the other person, but that he will discover what is right out of himself if I contribute something towards it.' Thoughts of this kind shed a quality of gentleness over the character and behaviour of the pupil, and *gentleness* is one of the main factors in all esoteric training. *Harshness* scares away from around you the soul-forms which should awaken your inner eyes; *gentleness* clears away the obstacles and opens your inner eyes.

Together with *gentleness*, another trait will soon be developed in the soul of the pupil—that of quietly *paying attention* to all the delicate features in the soul-life around him while maintaining *complete stillness* within his own soul. If an individual has achieved this, the emotions in his environment will work upon him in such a way that his own soul will grow, and in growing will develop an organic structure, just as a plant thrives in the sunlight. Gentleness and quiet inner patience open the soul to the soul-world, the spirit to the spirit-world: persevere in quiet seclusion; close the senses to the messages they brought you before your training; bring to stillness all the thoughts which were in the habit of surging up and down within you; become inwardly still and silent. Wait in patience, and then higher worlds will begin to fashion your eyes of soul and ears of spirit. You must not expect immediately to see and hear in the worlds of soul and spirit, for what you are doing is merely a contribution to the development of your higher senses. You will be able to use eyes of soul and ears of spirit only when you actually possess these senses. If you have persevered for a time in quiet seclusion, then go about your customary daily affairs, having imprinted deeply upon your mind the thought: 'Some day, when I am ready, I shall attain what I am destined to attain.' And strictly refrain from attempting by your own arbitrary will to draw any higher powers to yourself.

These are instructions which every pupil receives from his teacher at the beginning of the path he is to tread. If he obeys them, he achieves his goal; if he does not obey them, all labour is in vain. But they are difficult only for one who lacks patience and perseverance. There are no obstacles other than those which a person places *in his own path* and can avoid if he so resolves. This must be continually emphasized, because many people form an entirely false idea of the difficulties of the esoteric path. In a certain sense it is easier to take the first steps along this path than to get the better of the commonest everyday difficulties of life without esoteric training. Apart from this, only such things as are attended by no dangers of any kind to the health of soul and body will be recommended here.

There are other paths which lead more quickly to the goal, but what is here meant has nothing to do with them because they may have certain effects upon a person which an experienced occultist considers undesirable. As certain information about these paths is constantly finding its way to the public, express warning must be given against them. For reasons which only the initiated can understand, *these* paths can never be made publicly known in their real form. The fragments which come to light here and there can never lead to wholesome results but may easily undermine health, happiness and peace of mind. Anyone who does not want to entrust himself to dark, sinister powers, of whose real nature and origin he can know nothing, had better have nothing to do with such things.

Something may still be said about the environment in which the exercises of esoteric training should be undertaken, for this is not without importance. Yet the circumstances differ for almost every individual. Anyone who is practising the exercises in an environment imbued only with self-seeking interests, such as those which prevail in the modern struggle for existence, must be conscious of the fact that these interests are not without effect upon the develop-

ment of his organs of soul. It is true that the inner laws of
these organs are so powerful that no such influence can do
decisive harm. A lily can never grow into a thistle, however
inappropriate its environment; nor can the eye of the soul
ever become anything other than it is destined to be, even
when exposed to the self-seeking interests of modern cities.
But under all circumstances it is beneficial if the pupil now
and then surrounds himself with the restful peace, the
intrinsic virtue and grace of nature. Conditions are particu-
larly favourable for one whose esoteric training can be pursued in the midst of the green world of plants, or among the
sunny hills and the enchanted innocence of nature. This
environment draws out the inner organs in a harmony that
can never be achieved in a modern city. An individual who at
least during childhood was able to breathe the air perfumed
by the scent of fir trees, to gaze at snow-capped mountain
peaks and the peaceful life of woodland creatures and insects
is more fortunate than the city-dweller.

Yet no one who is obliged to live in a city should fail to
provide his developing organs of soul and spirit with the
nourishment afforded by the inspired teachings of spiritual
research. He whose eyes cannot watch the woods turning
green day by day in springtime should compensate by
imbuing his heart and soul with the sublime teachings of the
Bhagavad Gita, of St John's Gospel, of St Thomas à Kempis,
and the descriptive findings of spiritual science. There are
many paths to the summit of insight but a right choice is
essential. Concerning these the esotericist can say much that
will seem strange to the uninitiated. For example, someone
may be very far advanced on the path. He may be at the very

point where his eyes of soul and ears of spirit are about to open; and then he may be fortunate enough to journey across a calm or maybe a tempestuous sea, and a veil falls away from the eyes of his soul: suddenly he becomes a seer. Another is equally at the point where that veil needs only to be loosened and this will come about through some drastic stroke of destiny. Upon another individual such a stroke might well have the effect of paralysing his strength and undermining his energy; and then, for the esoteric pupil, this is what becomes the cause of his enlightenment. A third perseveres patiently for years without any perceptible results. Suddenly, while sitting peacefully in his room, spiritual light is all around him; the walls disappear, become transparent to his soul, and a new world stretches before his eyes that are now endowed with spiritual sight or resounds in his ears that are now open to spiritual hearing.

(*Knowledge of the Higher Worlds*, 1904–05)

9. Conversing with the Goddess Natura

We move in an entirely different direction spiritually[22] when we concentrate on certain different qualities of metal, of metallic substances. Just as we can do this with iron, tin or lead, so can we do it in connection with copper. We can concentrate on the metallic nature of copper, we can become one with copper in our soul-life, with its colour, with its consistency, with the strangely striated nature of its surface, in short with everything we can experience in our soul in connection with the metallic nature of copper. We then find ourselves being transported not into unconsciousness but into the opposite. We have a sense of becoming inwardly filled with something. We become more able to feel ourselves inwardly. We have a feeling that this copper, about which we are thinking with concentration, fills us from top to bottom, right into our very fingertips and into our skin. It fills us right up. It makes us full of something. And then we feel how whatever it is that fills us begins to ray outwards. It rays outwards from this central point beneath our heart into all the rest of our body. We feel as though we have a second body inside us, a second person. We feel internally squeezed. There is a slight pain which increases. We feel everything within us being inwardly squeezed.

But once again, we fill everything with this feeling of initiation, we feel as though there is a second human being within us. And with this initiate feeling we have the experience of being able to say: With my ordinary human being, the one I received through birth and upbringing, the one who accompanies me as I go about in the world, the one who looks out at the world through my eyes, the one with whom I hear, the one with whom I feel things, it is with this human being that I walk about. But because I have done the training, because I have done the exercises, I am now able to give this second person, the one who is squeezing me, the ability to perceive. This second human being will be rather strange. He has no separate eyes or ears; it is as though he is all eye and all ear. He is like a sense organ. He perceives with subtlety. He perceives things which we are otherwise unable to perceive. Suddenly the world becomes richer. And like a snake shedding its skin we can for a while, for a short while measured in seconds, we can experience a great deal with this second person who has formed inside us as the copper person, we can leave our body and move freely about the world in spirit. He can be separated from us, although it is painful and although the pain increases; he can be separated from our body.

We can emerge from this. And when we emerge we can experience more than when we remain inside. Above all, once we have reached this stage of being able to emerge, we are able to follow someone who has died into the world he will be entering after a few days. He has passed through the portal of death, and all the connections have ceased that we had with him as earthly human beings. He is cremated or buried. He is no longer present on the earth.

Once we go out of our body with the second human being I have been describing, we are able to continue following the soul who has passed through the portal of death. We remain united with that soul. And we experience how that soul, after passing through the portal of death, spends the first years and decades going backwards through his life. This becomes a truth for us. We can observe it. We can accompany the one who has died. We see what the dead person experienced here on the earth before he died; the first event he experiences is the one that occurred last; the event after that is the second to last, going all the way back. He lives his way back to his birth, taking one third of the duration of his life. If someone has reached the age of 60, he spends about 20 years going backwards through his whole life. And we can follow him in this.

(13 August 1924)

It is not a poetic image, dear friends,[23] but a true picture of reality that I want to present you with today. Let us imagine Alanus ab Insulis speaking to his pupils about Nature at the School of Chartres, where the beautiful cathedral still stands. Nature, he may say, is a being we can no longer comprehend, a being who withdraws from us as we approach her. Humanity has developed powers which lead elsewhere but are no longer capable of comprehending Nature in the way those with insight were able to comprehend her in ages past. Nature was a mighty and great spiritual being who was at work wherever rocks were formed in the mountains, wherever plants grew up out of the earth, wherever stars sparkled in the skies. In a wonderful womanly form an immeasurably great being was everywhere at work. That is what visionaries saw of old. And in keeping with what those ancients told, we can nowadays still imagine what Nature was: that force which was everywhere at work in warmth, in all phenomena of light, in all phenomena of colour, in all phenomena of life. Yet she withdraws from us when we endeavour to approach her. The goddess Natura lives and weaves in all things, a goddess, a divine, spiritual being about whom we know but whom we can only recognize if we can see her with spiritual vision.

In the twelfth century, a personage such as Alanus ab Insulis was still able to describe such matters to his pupils at the School of Chartres. But because this goddess Natura was seen to be disappearing into a haze together with all that was alive but which we now study only as abstract, dead laws of nature, she withdrew from us, and that is why the faces of those individuals developed such a tragic and sad expression.

And then there were individuals such as Dante's great teacher Brunetto Latini, who, owing to a special karmic situation, was afflicted while on a journey by a kind of sun-stroke which changed him so that in an altered state of consciousness he became able to perceive the goddess Natura, something which he describes in his book *Tesoretto*. (This was far more important to him than the pain he had felt when the Guelfs were driven out of his home town.) He describes vividly, with lively imagination, how he was passing through a dreary forest on the way to his home town of Florence. In that dreary forest he approached a hill upon which the goddess Natura was at work. And the goddess Natura explained to him how thinking, feeling and will work in the human soul, and also the meaning of the human being's four temperaments, and furthermore the significance of the human being's five senses.

This was a genuine schooling in spirit and soul, a reality which he underwent under the influence of that pathological condition which overcame him on his journey from Spain to his home town of Florence. He saw the weaving of the four elements of fire, earth, water and air; he saw the weaving of the planets and of the human soul in the starry heavens. All this he saw under the influence of the spiritual teaching vouchsafed him by the goddess Natura.

All this is told us by an individual of those times, but now described as best we can in the language of today. But one has the feeling that the quality of the knowledge possessed by those at work in olden times was quite different and that it always eludes us nowadays. One even has to be overcome by a pathological condition if one still wants to comprehend those secrets.

People in those days were certainly filled with a mighty urge to bring to life once more the true figure of the goddess Natura. In our own efforts to return with our human feeling and with our human thinking to that knowledge we have the impression: Well, even today we are confronted by nature, but we give it a name that is entirely abstract, an accumulation of laws. And we are pleased if we manage to create some sort of coherence in these laws. If we look back a few hundred years we see a living relationship between an individual and a divine being and how everything worked coherently, how the sun rose and the sun set, how the stones were warmed and how the plants were warmed, all in a living way. Consider what a different form of science that is! The science of those times encompassed the deeds of the goddess Natura. And how different was the mood of the students at Chartres—

mostly Cistercian monks—and then the mood today of students as they end their schooling. Things were certainly more alive, more essential then. And how alive and essential are descriptions such as that given by Brunetto Latini, Dante's great teacher.

We can well imagine how alive all that was, for all the wonderful images and figures depicted by Dante in his *Commedia* arose out of the lively descriptions stemming from his teacher Brunetto Latini who had been initiated as a result of a karmic situation. Similarly, much of what was taught at Chartres and elsewhere stemmed from initiates such as Joachim of Fiore and others.

In those days the use of the word 'Natura' was less abstract than it is today. It depicted something which was present in what the senses could experience externally but which withdrew, which eluded one. And there was something else as well, and I am not painting a poetic picture, for it is entirely real. Imagine yourself as an older student in a course being taught by Alanus ab Insulis. Imagine having attended the course and then set off for a walk with Alanus ab Insulis, all the while talking about what has been said. What would have happened?

A conversation like this would have been quite special. It would have been possible to speak of the goddess Natura who reveals to us the phenomena of the external, sense-perceptible world, but who also eludes us. Having become quite heated in this discussion about matters of the soul, one would feel a tap on one's shoulder from Alanus ab Insulis who would be saying: 'Alas, if only we were still able to sleep as people did in olden times. Then we would become acquainted with the other, the hidden side of the goddess Natura. But nowadays when we sleep we become unconscious, whereas in olden times the other side of nature would have been revealed to us. If we could still sleep clairvoyantly, as did those of old, then we would come to know the goddess Natura.' Yes, this is what Alanus ab Insulis would have said as he tapped us on the shoulder.

(*14 August 1924*)

When we step forward with the most advanced learning[24] attainable in any university faculty and with it approach the being who still exists as the goddess Natura about whom the teachers at the School of Chartres spoke, such teachers as Bernard Silvestris, Alanus ab Insulis and others, when we approach this being we discover that our present-day knowledge appears to be somewhat inadequate. We have to say to ourselves: In keeping with present-day knowledge and science I know only about what is relevant to the world in which I live between birth and death; this is no longer relevant once I enter even into the closest spiritual sphere with my consciousness and become able to go beyond death in following those who have died.

We learn about chemistry. But what we learn in chemistry is valid only for the world in which we live between birth and death. Nothing in chemistry has any meaning in a world into which we can follow those who have died after their death. Everything we learn here in the physical world has no meaning for that other world; it has no significance and is merely a memory once we have entered that world. And as soon as we enter that world it opens up for us and we feel how the everyday world in which we learned so much begins to disappear. It is that other world which immediately opens up.

Imagine a mountain in the world where we live between birth and death. The mountain certainly appears quite dense to us. We see it in the distance. It reflects towards us the light it receives from the sun. We see its forms and contours. We approach it, getting ever closer to it. We feel how it resists us when we step onto it. It gives us the impression of being real. But now imagine we are in another world. Everything we described as being solid now ceases to have any meaning. There is something which seems to appear from out of the mountain, growing ever larger and larger. And this gives us the impression of another reality.

Or imagine we see a cloud above the mountain as we stand here in our everyday world. We are convinced that it consists of condensed vapour. It, too, ceases to have any reality. Something entirely different emerges from this cloud. What emerges gradually unites with the disappearing cloud and mountain; something new emerges—a new reality which is more than mere mist, for it has a proper shape. And this applies to all things. We see many things here, for example many people. As soon as they enter into the spiritual world their sharp contours disappear. Dear ladies, you will have to bring yourselves to realize that all your pretty dresses will no longer be seen. Instead, what will appear of all those seated here will be something belonging to soul and spirit. What will appear is that which is mysteriously at work in the air and in all our surroundings. A new world comes into being, and this is the world in which those who have died find themselves.

And then we become aware of something else. We notice something else. If this world into which we have now entered did not exist, if this world were not also present wherever the world exists which we experience between birth and death, we would, as human beings, have no eyes and no ears or indeed any senses at all. The world described by the chemist or the physicist cannot provide us with any senses. We would be entirely without senses, we would be blind and deaf. Our senses would not come into being in us.

This is what was so surprising when Brunetto Latini—having travelled from Spain and reached the vicinity of his home city of Florence and been overcome by that slight sunstroke—entered into that other world. That was when he noticed: I have my senses from this other world. As a human being I would be without senses if this other world were not to penetrate over into the world in which I normally see what is around me. So as a human being I am connected with that second world as a result of my senses having been put into my body.

In all ages, that second world has been spoken of as the world of the elements. In that world it is meaningless to talk of oxygen, hydrogen, nitrogen and so on. We can talk of these while we live between birth and death. But in that other world it is meaningful to speak of the elements of earth, water, air, fire and light, for there is no connection between our senses and the specifics of hydrogen, oxygen and so on. When we talk of the aroma of violets or of asafoetida,[25] saying that the one is lovely while the other is disgusting, there is no point in a chemist specifying the chemical substances involved, for that is meaningless. On the contrary, everything at work in aromas is filled with spirit. As regards the world into which a person initially enters after death one should rather speak of them as being of the air, of an air that is nuanced and everywhere filled with spirit. So our senses are rooted in the world of the elements, in the world where one can still meaningfully speak of earth, water, fire, air.

An erroneous idea here confronts an accurate idea. What is the attitude of a modern philosopher who, having superseded the naivety inherent in the ideas of earlier ages, regards himself as being reasonable and sensible? He says: 'Well, the conceptions of former times were crude. They spoke only approximately about the elements of earth, water, fire and air. We, on the other hand, now know that there are 70 or 80 elements, not merely four or five.'

If an ancient Greek were to come back to the earth—not through reincarnation, but as he was in those times—and find himself confronted with this statement, he would say: 'Well yes, you do indeed have your oxygen, your hydrogen and so on, these are your elements. But you have forgotten what *we* had in *our* four elements. You have forgotten this. You no longer know anything about it. But no senses would ever arise out of all your 72 or 75 elements, for it is out of the four elements that the senses arise. Therefore it was we, in our time, who knew more about the human being. We knew how this external, peripheral realm, which is permeated by the senses, comes to be formed within the human being.'

We, today, can only appreciate the impressions received by those who had come close to initiation, as was the case with Brunetto Latini, if we take the state of their soul into consideration, if we take into account their surprised acceptance of such startling revelations. It is of course initially shocking to be told that what we had thought to be reality, in what our eyes see or what our ears hear, would of itself have been incapable of creating an eye or an ear at all but that this was done instead by what I have been describing as the reality behind these things.

The most important thing to learn is that we cannot possibly reach such knowledge by confronting nature in the torpid manner to which we have grown accustomed. Everything becomes alive as soon as we enter into that other world. We say to ourselves: Yes, that hill with which we are familiar is dead. We were not aware that something in it was alive. But something does indeed live in it, and here it is. That cloud, it appeared dead to us. But now what lives in it, which formerly we did not notice, is becoming apparent. Everything comes alive. Essential beings are alive in this living and weaving.

We do not bring forth the laws of nature out of our brain. We are confronted by a spiritual being, the Being Natura who tells us these things and shows us these things, whose messages are a reality. It becomes a reality that we communicate with beings from a supersensible world about facts that are all around us. We thus move away from what is merely abstract in the laws about the world and enter into what is alive in it; instead of fabricating the laws of nature by means of experimenting with ideas, we come to feel ourselves confronted by beings from another world who tell us what we need to know because they understand that these are things which we as human beings must learn about.

In this way we enter in the right way into the spiritual worlds. We come to realize that if we did indeed possess nothing but our senses, our eyes with their optic nerves, our nose with its olfactory nerves, our ears with their auditory nerves, these would merely point backwards, and we would never come to the realization that oxygen, hydrogen, nitrogen and so on even exist, that they exist and can be perceived by us in the period between our birth and our death. We would instead be looking into the world of the elements, finding earth, water, air and fire everywhere. And differences in the degree of solidity or earthiness, or of liquidity or wateriness, would be as uninteresting for us as is small change for a millionaire. We would simply not be interested in all that.

As sensory individuals we know about the elemental world through our nerves which emanate from our senses. And as soon as we become aware of what I have been describing we also become aware that in us as human beings our sensory nerves go backwards, become more differentiated and further honed so that something else is formed, namely our brain. We then no longer enter further into ourselves but become more outward, adding to the four elements of earth, fire, water and air those other aspects which we learn about in addition between being born and dying.

This brain, which is turned outwards from the backward-facing optic nerves, auditory nerves and so on, this brain to which as human beings we attach such value, has a meaning only between birth and death. This brain inside our skull is significant solely for our life on earth. For the spiritual world it is the most insignificant of all. Therefore the brain has to be deactivated when we want to enter even only into the world next to ours. The brain has to be switched off. It is a dreadful obstacle for higher insight. Once the brain is switched off one then has to live again in the senses, the senses into which the newly awakened spiritual element has been pressed. And thereby one enters into Imagination. Normally the senses perceive the sensory images of the external, physical world, and the brain then transforms them into abstract thoughts, those dead, abstract thoughts. If one then disconnects the brain, thus living once again in the senses, then one experiences everything as Imaginations. It is of this that we become aware. And this shows us that through immersing ourselves more deeply into life situations we develop states of consciousness which are higher than those we have in ordinary life.

Our senses, which of course lie at the surface of our body, our eyes, our ears, constantly perceive our world [see drawing, red]. Here we stand, dear friends. Our senses, which lie on our surface, perceive this world of the elements.

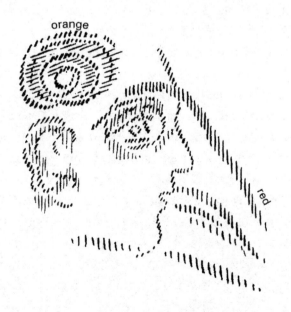

They also still see the dead in that world, even years after they have died. That all of this is extinguished is the result of the brain being behind the senses [orange]. Here I stand with my brain and my senses. This human being, who resides on my external surface, sees the spiritual world within, and he sees the dead there during the years that follow their death. But my brain extinguishes all this; it extinguishes earth, water, fire, air; and I look at the sharp contours of what is present as the physical world, what is present only for the world in which I live between my birth and my death. Quite another world exists over there, but I extinguish it through my brain while looking at the world which is familiar to us as the world of ordinary consciousness.

For modern individuals, then, we have the meditation about which I spoke yesterday. For people in former times there also existed, in keeping with that meditation, the imbibing of certain metallic substances as I described yesterday. In order to enter into the next stage of consciousness, one has to eliminate brain consciousness and immerse oneself with one's spirit in the consciousness possessed by our eyes and ears. Animals also possess this consciousness, for they have not developed their brain physically behind their senses. It is just that they do not possess a soul which is endowed with an ego; so they cannot with their spirit immerse themselves in their senses. They immerse themselves only with their unsubtle soul and therefore do not see what the human being can see in his surroundings when he immerses himself in his senses with his spirit.

(15 August 1924)

10. Understanding Life as a Process of Breathing

The conditions for embarking on esoteric training have not been arbitrarily determined.[26] They arise from the essential nature of esoteric knowledge. Just as no one who refuses to handle a paintbrush can become a painter, so too can no one receive esoteric training who is unwilling to fulfil the demands considered necessary by teachers. Fundamentally speaking, the teacher can give nothing except advice, and everything he says should be accepted in this sense. He has already passed through the preparatory paths to knowledge of the higher worlds and knows from experience what is necessary. It rests entirely upon the *free will* of each individual whether he chooses to tread the same paths or not. Were anyone to demand that a teacher should admit him to esoteric training without his having fulfilled the conditions, this would be equivalent to saying: 'Teach me how to paint but do not ask me to handle a paintbrush.'

The teacher can offer nothing unless the would-be recipient comes to meet him of his own free will. But it must be emphasized that a general wish for higher knowledge is not sufficient. Many people, of course, will have this wish, but nothing can be achieved by it *alone* as long as the *special* conditions attached to esoteric training are not accepted. This point should be considered by those who complain that esoteric training is not going to be easy for them. Failure or unwillingness to fulfil the strict conditions *must for the time being* entail the abandonment of esoteric training. True, the conditions are *strict*, but they are not *rigid*, because the fulfilment of them not only should be, but actually must be, a free deed.

If this fact is overlooked, the conditions of esoteric training may easily seem to involve a coercion of the soul or the conscience; for the training is based upon development of the *inner* life and the teacher must therefore give corresponding advice. But nothing that is required to arise out of free decision can be interpreted as compulsion. If someone asks the teacher, 'Tell me your secrets but leave me with my accustomed emotions, feelings and thoughts,' that is an unrealistic demand. The person simply wants to satisfy his curiosity and desire for knowledge. With this attitude of mind, higher knowledge can never be attained.

We will now consider in sequence the conditions to be observed by the pupil. It must be emphasized that the *complete* fulfilment of any one of these conditions is not demanded, but only the *endeavour* to fulfil them. No one can *wholly* fulfil the conditions, but everyone can set out on the path towards their fulfilment. All that matters is the effort of will, the setting of the mind to enter upon this path.

The first condition is that heed should be paid to the furtherance of bodily and spiritual *health*. Health does not, of course, primarily depend upon the individual; but everyone can make the effort to improve in this respect. Healthy knowledge can come only from healthy human beings. In esoteric training an unhealthy individual is not rejected, but it must be demanded of the pupil that he has the will to lead a healthy life. In this respect he must achieve the greatest possible independence. The well-meaning advice of others, given—mostly unsought—to everyone, is as a rule quite superfluous. Each individual must endeavour to take care of himself.

In a physical respect it will be more a matter of warding off harmful influences than of anything else. In order to carry out our duties we must often undertake things that are not conducive to our health. When it is right to do so, one must give preference to duty rather than to the care of health. Just think how many things can be more important than health, often indeed more important than life itself; but for the esoteric pupil this should *never* apply to *pleasure*. For him, pleasure can be only a *means* towards health and life. And here, above all, everyone must be honest and truthful with himself. And it is useless to lead an ascetic life when the underlying motives are the same as in other indulgences. Someone may derive satisfaction from asceticism as someone else does from wine-drinking, but he cannot hope that asceticism of this kind will help him to attain higher knowledge.

Many ascribe to their station in life everything that apparently prevents them from making progress in this respect. They say: 'In the present conditions of my life I cannot develop.' For other reasons it may be desirable for many to change their stations in life, but no one need do so for the purpose of esoteric training. He need do only as much as is possible, whatever his position, to further the health of his body and soul. Every kind of work can be of service to mankind as a whole; and it is a much greater achievement of the soul to realize how necessary for mankind is a trivial, perhaps even an unpleasant employment than to think: 'This work is not good enough for me; I am destined for something better.'

Of special importance for the pupil is the striving for a completely healthy mind. An unhealthy life of feeling and thought will in every case obstruct the paths to higher knowledge. Clear, calm thinking, and stability of feeling and emotion are the fundamentals here. Nothing should be farther from the pupil than any tendency to a fancy-ridden, excitable life, to nervous tension, exaltation and fanaticism: he should acquire a healthy outlook on all circumstances in life; he should find his bearings in life with assurance; he should quietly let things work upon him and speak to him. He should be at pains to meet the demands of life in all necessary directions. All exaggerated, one-sided tendencies in his judgement and feeling should be avoided. If this condition were not fulfilled he would find his way into worlds of his own imagination instead of higher worlds; instead of truth, his own pet opinions would assert themselves. It is better for the pupil to be 'matter-of-fact' than excitable and full of fancies.

The second condition is to feel oneself *a member* of humanity as a whole. A great deal is included in the fulfilment of this condition, but each individual can fulfil it only in his own way. If I am a teacher and a pupil is not what I would wish him to be, I should not direct my feeling primarily against him but against myself. I should feel at one with my pupil to the extent of asking myself: 'Is his shortcoming not the result of my own action?' Instead of directing my feeling against him, I shall then far rather reflect upon how I should myself behave in order that he may in future be better able to satisfy my expectations. Such an attitude gradually brings about a change in the whole of a person's way of thinking. This holds good in all things, the smallest and the greatest alike. With this attitude of mind I shall see a criminal, for example, differently. I suspend my judgement and say to myself: 'I am a human being just as he is. The education which circumstances made possible for me *may alone* have saved me from his fate.' I shall then certainly arrive at the thought that this human brother would have become a different man if the teachers who took pains with me had bestowed the same care upon him. I shall reflect that something was given to me which was withheld from him, that I owe my good fortune to the circumstance that it was withheld from him. And then it will no longer be difficult for me to think that I am only a member of humanity as a whole and *share responsibility* for everything that occurs. This does not imply that such a thought should be immediately translated into outer agitation. It should rather be tended in stillness within the soul. Then, quite gradually, it will set its mark upon the outward bearing of a person. In such matters each one has to begin by reforming himself. It is of no avail to make general demands of humanity in the sense of the foregoing thoughts. It is easy to decide what people ought to be; but the pupil works in the depths, not on the surface. It would therefore be quite wrong to connect the demand of the esoteric teacher indicated here with any external, let alone political, demand with which spiritual training can have nothing to do. Political agitators 'know', as a rule, what to 'demand' of other people; but they seldom speak of demands on themselves.

The third condition in esoteric training is directly connected with what has been said above. The pupil must be able to work his way to the realization that his thoughts and feelings are as important for the world as his actions. He must recognize that it is just as harmful to hate a fellow being as to strike him. The knowledge then comes to me that when I strive to improve myself I accomplish something not only for myself but also for the world. The world derives as much benefit from my unsullied feelings and thoughts as from my good conduct. As long as I cannot believe in this importance of my inner life for the world I am not fit to be an esoteric pupil. I shall be imbued with the right belief in the significance of my inner self, of my soul, when I work at it as though it were at least as real as anything external. I must come to admit that every feeling has as real an effect as an action of my hand.

Herewith the fourth condition is already indicated: to become convinced that the real being of man lies not in the outer world but in the inner world. Anyone who regards himself as a product merely of the outer world, as an outcome of the physical world, can achieve nothing in esoteric training, for to feel oneself a being of soul and spirit is its very basis. Someone who acquires this feeling is able to distinguish between inner duty and outward success. He learns to recognize that the one cannot be directly measured by the other. The esoteric pupil must find the mean between what is prescribed by external conditions and the conduct he recognizes as right for himself. He should not force upon his environment anything for which it can have no understanding; but he must also be quite free from the desire to do only what his environment will accept. Recognition of the truths for which he stands must be sought *only* in the voice of his own soul, with its genuine striving for knowledge. But he must *learn* as much as he possibly can from his environment in order to discover what will benefit those around him and be useful to them. In this way he will develop what is known in spiritual science as a 'spiritual balance'. An 'open heart' for the needs of the outer world lies on one of the scales and 'inner resoluteness and unswerving endurance' on the other.

This points to the fifth condition: steadfastness in carrying out a resolution once it is taken. Nothing should induce the pupil to deviate from a resolution he has taken, except the insight that he is wrong. Every resolution is a force, and even if this force does not have immediate success at the point where it is applied it nevertheless works on in its own way. Success is decisive only if an action arises from desire. But all such actions are worthless in face of the higher world. There, *love* for an action is alone decisive. Everything that impels the pupil to action should find expression in *love*. Then he will never weary in his efforts to translate a resolution into deed, however often he may fail. And in this way he reaches the stage of not waiting to see the *outward* effect of his deeds, but of being content with what they are in themselves. He will learn to offer up his deeds, even his whole being, to the world, no matter how the world may receive his sacrifice. Anyone who wishes to become an esoteric pupil must resolve to be ready for a life of sacrifice.

A sixth condition is the development of a feeling of *thankfulness* for everything that falls to man's lot. We must realize that our own existence is a gift from the whole universe. How much is needed in order that each one of us may receive and sustain our existence! How much do we not owe to nature and to other human beings! Those who wish for esoteric training must incline to such thoughts. He who is incapable of lending himself to them is also incapable of developing the *all-embracing love* that is necessary for the attainment of higher knowledge. Something that I do not love cannot reveal itself to me. And every revelation must fill me with thankfulness, for I am the richer for it.

All these conditions must unite in the seventh: to grasp life constantly in the way demanded by these conditions. The pupil is thus enabled to give his life a uniform character. All the ways of expressing himself will be brought into harmony with each other and no longer be contradictory. He will be prepared for the inner tranquillity he must achieve during the first steps of esoteric training.

Anyone who has the sincere and genuine will to fulfil these conditions may decide to undertake esoteric training. He will then be ready to follow the advice indicated above. Much of this advice may appear superficial to many people and they will perhaps say that they had expected the training to take less strict *forms*. But everything inward must come to expression outwardly. And as little as a picture is really there when it exists only in the mind of the artist, as little can any esoteric training be without outward expression. Disregard for strict forms is shown only by those who do not know that the internal must come to expression in the external. True, it is the *spirit* of a thing that matters, not the form; but just as the form without the spirit is null and void, so would the spirit remain inactive if it did not create a form for itself.

The conditions are designed to render the pupil strong enough to meet the further demands that his training will unavoidably make upon him. If he fails to fulfil these conditions, he will be hesitant and apprehensive when faced with every new demand. He will lack the faith in man that is necessary for him. All striving for truth must be founded upon faith in and true love for humanity. This must be its *foundation*, but *not* its origin; striving for truth can flow only from the soul's own power. And the love of man must widen gradually into love for all beings—indeed for all existence. Anyone who fails to fulfil the above conditions will lack both the genuine love for everything that builds and creates, and the inclination to refrain from all destructiveness. The pupil must become a person who never destroys anything for the sake of destruction, not only in his actions but also in his words, feelings and thoughts. He must delight in growth, in development, and he must lend his hand to destruction only when he is able, through and from out of destruction, to promote new life. This does not mean that he must look on passively while evil runs riot but rather that even in what is evil he must look for those aspects through which he may transform it into good. He will then see more and more clearly that evil and imperfection are best combated by the creation of the perfect and the good. The pupil knows that out of empty nothingness nothing can be created, but also that the imperfect can be transformed into the perfect. Anyone who develops within himself the propensity for creative activity will soon find himself to be capable of dealing with evil in the right way.

Anyone who embarks upon esoteric training must realize

that its purpose is to build, not to destroy; the pupil should therefore bring with him the will for sincere and devoted work, not for criticism and destructiveness. He must be capable of *reverence*, for he has to learn what he does not yet know; he should have reverence for whatever discloses itself to him. Work and reverence: these are the fundamental demands made upon the pupil. Many a one will have to realize that he is making no progress in his training, although in his own opinion he is indefatigably active. The reason is that he has not rightly grasped the nature of work and reverence. Work undertaken for the sake of success will be the least successful, and learning pursued without devotion will bring the least progress. *Love* of the work itself, not of success—this alone leads to progress. And if the learner is trying to develop healthy thinking and sound judgement, he need not invalidate his devotion through doubt and distrust.

Nobody need be reduced to servile dependence by listening to information with quiet reverence and attention, instead of at once countering it with his own opinion. Those who have acquired a certain amount of higher knowledge know that they owe everything to quiet attentiveness and patient reflection, not to wilful personal judgement. We should always bear in mind that there is no need to learn anything that we are already capable of evaluating. If, therefore, we want *only* to judge, we can learn nothing more. In esoteric training, however, it is learning that matters. We should desire with heart and soul to be learners. If there is something we cannot understand, it is better not to judge at all than to judge negatively. Understanding can be left until later.

The higher we climb the steps of knowledge, the more necessary is this quiet, reverent listening. All perception of truth, all life and action in the world of the spirit are subtle and delicate in comparison with the functions of the ordinary intellect and the business of life in the physical world. The wider our horizon becomes, the more delicate are the activities we have to undertake. It is because of this that people arrive at such different 'opinions' and 'points of view' regarding higher spheres. But there is in reality only *one* opinion regarding higher truths, and this *one* opinion is within reach of everyone who through work and devotion has risen to the stage where he can actually behold the truth. A view that differs from the one true view can be arrived at only when someone, insufficiently prepared, judges in accordance with his pet ideas, his habitual thoughts, and so forth. Just as there is only one valid opinion about a mathematical theorem, so is it with the things of the higher worlds.

But before anyone can reach an 'opinion' of this kind, he must have undergone a proper preparation for doing so. If this were duly recognized, the conditions made by the teacher in esoteric training would surprise no one. It is absolutely correct that truth and the higher life abide in every human soul and that each individual can and must find them *for himself*. But they lie deeply buried and can be brought up from the depths only after all obstacles have been cleared away. Only those with experience can advise how this may be done. Spiritual science gives such advice. It forces no truth on anyone, proclaims no dogma; but it shows a way. It is true that everyone could also find this way unaided, but perhaps only after many incarnations. The way is shortened by esoteric training. Through it an individual can more quickly reach a point where he can cooperate in those worlds where the salvation and evolution of mankind are furthered through spiritual activity.

(*Knowledge of the Higher Worlds*, 1904/1905)

11. Conclusion: Devotion and Love

An individual who feels himself to be a free being when he is close to Michael is one who is on his way to imbuing his 'whole being' with the power of the intellect.[27] Although he thinks with his head, his heart feels the light and the dark of that thinking; and his will beams out his being when he allows the thoughts to weave within him as intentions. The individual becomes ever more human when he becomes an expression of the world; he finds himself not by *searching* for himself but by wilfully uniting in love with the world.

If he succumbs to the temptations of Ahriman while developing his freedom, the individual is dragged into an intellectuality as though into spiritual automatism; he becomes a construct and is no longer *himself*. The whole of his thinking becomes an experience of the head. This removes it from being an experience of his heart or of his life of will, thus extinguishing his individuality. By becoming a mere depiction of himself the individual loses more and more of what expresses his true inner being; he loses himself by *searching* for himself; he withdraws himself from the world by withholding his love from the world, whereas actually the individual only truly experiences *himself* when he loves the world.

What has been described here has shown how Michael leads us to Christ. In all the gravity of his being, of his attitude, of his actions, Michael moves in love through the world. By truly adhering to him one cultivates *love in one's relationship with the external world*. Love must first develop in a relationship with the external world, otherwise it becomes self-love.

When love is present through this attitude towards Michael, then *love for the other* will be able to shine back into one's own self. This self will then be able to love without loving itself. It is on paths of love like this that the human soul can find Christ.

When someone adheres to Michael he cultivates love with regard to the external world, and through this he finds *that* relationship with the inner world of his soul which will lead him to Christ.

In the age now beginning, there will be a need for humanity to pay attention to a world that is a spiritual world felt to be immediately adjacent to the physical world; this is where one will be able to find what has here been described as the Michael Being and the Michael Mission. *That* world which the individual describes as nature, when he looks at this physical world, is not the world in which he actually lives; it is a world which lies as far *beneath* the true world of humanity as the world of Michael lies *above* it. The individual, however, does not notice how, unconsciously, when he creates an inner image of his world, what actually comes into being is an image of a different world. In the very act of creating this image he is already busy excluding himself as he falls into the grip of spiritual automatism. The individual can only safeguard his humanity when he confronts *this* image of himself as an observer of nature with that *other* image of one who sees the world where Michael holds sway, where Michael points to the paths that lead to Christ.

(*Anthroposophical Leading Thoughts*, 1924)

Notes

1. These four maxims are quoted in *Mantric Sayings. Meditations* (CW 268). In 1907, during the Munich Congress, these maxims were spoken with reference to the two columns J(akim) and B(oas) situated in front of the stage. In that they correspond to the Tree of Knowledge and the Tree of Life they are connected with the legend of Paradise. See also the lecture of 21 May 1907 in *Rosicrucianism Renewed* (CW 284).

2. In *Knowledge of the Higher Worlds*, Steiner describes the development of various capacities in connection with the relevant organs, the so-called lotus flowers or chakras. With regard to the capacity of reverence and devotion, or mindfulness, which is especially emphasized in the present volume, it is above all the twelve-petalled lotus flower or heart chakra with which we are concerned. For the development of thinking, which Steiner considered essential for a modern schooling path, a 'provisional centre comes about in the head'. The 16-petalled lotus flower, the chakra of the larynx, then follows on from this as the schooling proceeds. 'A simple start is made, designed above all to deepen and intensify intelligent, rational thinking. This thinking is thereby made free and independent of all physical sense-impressions and experiences. It is concentrated, as it were, in a single point which is entirely under the person's control. Thereby a provisional centre is created for the currents of the ether body. This centre is not yet in the region of the heart, but in the head, and to the clairvoyant it appears as the starting point of movements. The only esoteric training that can be completely successful is one which first

creates this centre. If the centre were formed in the region of the heart from the very beginning, the incipient clairvoyant might certainly have glimpses of the higher worlds but he would have no true insight into the connection of these higher worlds with our physical world. And this is an unconditional necessity for human beings at the present stage of evolution. The clairvoyant must not become a fancy-ridden visionary; he *must* keep solid ground under his feet.' See *Knowledge of the Higher Worlds*, Chapter 6, 'Some Effects of Initiation'. In this connection we should note Steiner's premise that the three lotus flowers mentioned develop simultaneously and not sequentially.

3. See Johannes Schneider *Meditation in der asiatischen Kultur und in der Anthroposophie* (2010) regarding Buddhism in India, which experiences the world as an illusion (*maya*), and in China and Japan, where for the most part Zen Buddhism refers to the world of the senses.

4. For the statements referred to regarding new faculties of perception among future generations see *The Reappearance of the Christ in the Etheric* (CW 118).

5. The Rosicrucianism of Goethe mentioned here has been described and discussed especially by Frank Teichmann (1937–2006) in his final work *Goethe und die Rosenkreuzer* (Stuttgart 2007). See also the collection of lectures by Rudolf Steiner *Anthroposophie und Rosenkreuzertum* (Dornach 2007).

6. Lecture in Berlin on 28 October 1909 (in *The Spiritual Being of Art*, CW 58). This text is from the lecture entitled 'The Mission of Reverence', the third in a sequence in which Rudolf Steiner describes ways of training the three soul members, the sentient soul, the intellectual or mind soul, and here the consciousness soul.

7. This extract from *Knowledge of the Higher Worlds* (Chapter 2, Preparation) describes the first of the three stages of the schooling path published in written form by Rudolf Steiner for the first time in 1904/1905. The three stages are here described as 'Preparation', 'Enlightenment' and 'Initiation'. This account initially appeared in essay form in the journal *Lucifer-Gnosis* and then, from 1909 in book form. In other descriptions, for example *The Stages of Higher Knowledge*, which enlarges on *Knowledge of the Higher Worlds*, the stages described are always termed 'Imagination', 'Inspiration' and 'Intuition'. However, in all subsequent editions of *Knowledge of the Higher Worlds* (during Steiner's lifetime up to the 11th edition in 1922), the description of the schooling path given here was retained. The section 'Enlightenment' which follows 'Preparation' in the book, is included later in this present collection (see Chapter 5).

8. Lecture in Dornach on 27 May 1922, in *Life of the Human Soul* (CW 212). This passage gives an especially clear description of the difference between the old and the new yoga paths. It is of central importance for an understanding of the exercises in perception given in the anthroposophical schooling path because it shows the importance Steiner attaches to the development of thinking through perception. Thinking itself becomes an organ of perception resembling a basin into which the spiritual content can be poured. One very good example of the 'outer rhythm' described here is Rudolf Steiner's *Calendar of the Soul*. See also the lecture of 1 June 1922 in *The Tension between East and West*, CW 83.

9. Lecture in Helsingfors (Helsinki) on 3 April 1912, in *Spiritual Beings in the Heavenly Bodies and in the Kingdoms of Nature* (CW 136). The exercises in perception selected here introduce

a lecture cycle given by Steiner at the request of Finnish and Russian members of the Theosophical Society. The cycle is concerned with the hierarchies but especially also with the realms of the elemental beings. The exercises quoted introduce the schooling needed in order to gain perception of elemental beings.

10. Lecture in Dornach on 30 November 1919 in *Michael's Mission* (CW 194). In the first half of this lecture Rudolf Steiner spoke about earlier stages of cultural evolution and their influence in the world; in this connection he also discussed the way in which breathing was observed in the culture of yoga.

11. Steiner is here drawing attention to the edition of Goethe's *Theory of Colour* which he himself edited. 'When one looks at a dazzling yet colourless image it makes a strong impression and, as it fades, colour appears.' And in a footnote, Steiner points out: 'All after-images, of whatever kind, fade away in colours. Even though this has not yet been explained anatomically, it does show that the overall spectrum ... is prefigured in the eye.' (Johann Wolfgang von Goethe, *Scientific Studies*, Suhrkamp Publishers, 1988.) In this lecture Steiner is clearly referring to Goethe's phenomenalism, which Goethe himself described as follows: 'It is most important to grasp that everything factual is at the same time theoretical. The blue of the sky reveals the basic law of chromatics to us. There is no need to search for anything behind the phenomena; they themselves are the phenomenon.'

12. Lecture in Dornach on 22 December 1922, in *Man and the World of the Stars* (CW 219). In this lecture, which is included here in full, Steiner explains and adds to what he said about the 'light-soul-process' discussed in his lecture of 30 November

1919, clarifying further what is meant by a breathing process connected to an experience of the senses.

The lectures (from *Geist und Stoff, Leben und Tod*, GA 66) which contain the three passages quoted in this chapter are included in English as an appendix in *The Foundations of Human Experience*, CW 293).

13. Lecture in Berlin on 15 March 1917.

14. Lecture in Berlin on 17 March 1917.

15. Lecture in Berlin on 17 March 1917. These three passages are quoted from public lectures in which Rudolf Steiner spoke for the first time about his discovery of the threefold nature of the human organism. Indeed he spoke here in much greater detail than had been possible for him in the written descriptions in his book *Riddles of the Soul* (Mercury Press, 1996). He here clarifies in a unique way the connection between perception and the etheric and between feeling and the breathing process. It is upon these insights that the perception exercises and meditations given in *Knowledge of the Higher Worlds* are based.

16. This passage 'Enlightenment' from *Knowledge of the Higher Worlds* directly follows the text quoted in our chapter 'The Preparation'. In the original, however, the section 'Enlightenment' continues beyond what we have quoted here, and this is then also followed by the third section: 'Initiation'. To gain a full overview of these passages it would be helpful to refer to *Knowledge of the Higher Worlds*. Our purpose here was to select passages focused on the exercises appropriate for elementary, simple sensory experiences which in themselves form a unified whole. We should also point out that in *Knowledge of the Higher Worlds*, Chapter 6, 'Some Effects of Initiation', Steiner refers to a number of further exercises which should also be practised as part of a regular and healthy training for the development of

supersensible perception. These 'subsidiary exercises', as he called them, are described in detail in the relevant chapter. They comprise the so-called 'eightfold path' and the so-called 'six characteristics'. Regarding the six characteristics see Rudolf Steiner, *Six Steps in Self-Development, The Supplementary Exercises*, edited by Ates Baydur, Rudolf Steiner Press, 2010, and *Enlivening the Chakra of the Heart* by Florin Lowndes, Rudolf Steiner Press, 2010, and also *Das Leben Meistern. Zur Praxis des achtgliedrigen Pfads* by Adam Bittleston, Stuttgart 2002.

17. Lecture in Dornach on 2 October 1920, in *The Boundaries of Natural Science* (CW 322).

18. Lecture in Dornach on 3 October 1920 (evening) (CW 322). The two lectures from which the two passages here are quoted were given by Rudolf Steiner during the earliest Anthroposophical Schooling Course, held at the first Goetheanum. For the first, and only, time he here describes how the exercises from *Knowledge of the Higher Worlds*, which lead to Imagination and which in our present volume have been discussed in Chapter 1, 'The Preparation' and Chapter 5, 'The Enlightenment', can be further developed for those who have been scientifically educated (which nowadays includes most people who have received a more advanced education). In these exercises, pure thinking is developed but then suspended to enable the individual to proceed to pure perception. Pure perception is the foundation for practically all the perception exercises described in *Knowledge of the Higher Worlds*. At the end of this second passage, Steiner refers once more to the breathing process, describing thinking and perceiving as a higher form of breathing, which he had earlier termed the 'light-soul-process'.

Here we are given a more detailed description as to which senses are involved with Imagination. It is with the lower senses, those which are developed during the first seven years of life, that we are concerned. Perception is developed consciously in a scientific way, so that one gains an intensity of feeling otherwise only experienced unconsciously by the small child.

19. Lecture in Dornach on 23 November 1923, in *Mystery Knowledge and Mystery Centres* (CW 232).

20. Ibid. As with the lecture from the Anthroposophical Schooling Course quoted previously, Rudolf Steiner described, in the first part of this lecture, not reproduced here, the experience of pure thinking. At this point, where the experience of thinking is described, the thinking leads on into the experience of feeling, just as in the previous lecture it led on to pure perception. In this second extract from the lecture the description of remembering continues. As with the lecture from the Schooling Course, Steiner is here concerned with an enhancement of perception and thus with an enhancement of the human being's relationship with the environment and with nature.

The process of becoming detached from oneself is described for the first time in *Knowledge of the Higher Worlds* as being a fundamental component of the schooling path. It can be attained by the regular practice of looking backwards over the day just passed while regarding oneself as a stranger. See also *Strengthening the Will*, ed. Martina Maria Sam, Rudolf Steiner Press, 2010. The experience of remembering becomes the foundation for a more intensive experience of nature based on feelings.

21. This extract from *Knowledge of the Higher* Worlds (in Chapter 4, 'Practical Aspects') is linked directly with the description of

the exercises in 'Preparation', 'Enlightenment' and 'Initiation'. The fundamental importance of controlling the life of feeling is especially emphasized with respect to the development of higher forms of knowledge and an exact clairvoyance.

22. Lecture in Torquay on 13 August 1924, *True and False Paths in Spiritual Investigation* (CW 243).

23. Lecture in Torquay on 14 August 1924, (ibid).

24. Lecture in Torquay on 15 August 1924, (ibid).

Regarding the meditation referred to at the end of this extract from the lecture of 15 August, Rudolf Steiner had also said the following in the previous day's lecture (14 August):

> You see, the sole correct way for today is for the individual, as I said yesterday, to become familiar with nature in his soul. As regards the nature of copper, he must develop a keen sense for the colour of copper, for what it is like when one grinds it down, for its effect in copper vitriol and the acid it contains, and so on. When an individual gains a feeling for it in this way and now meditates on that feeling, it will work upon him in the right way.
>
> You might now say: That's all very well, but in your book *Knowledge of the Higher Worlds* you never mentioned copper or that one must immerse oneself in copper in this way. You are quite right, I did not. But other things are certainly mentioned there, not with reference to copper, but in connection with other things. I described there how one must immerse oneself in the nature of crystals, of plants and so on. These elementary exercises are indeed discussed. There is no mention specifically of learning about the nature of copper; one would have to write a whole library of books if one were to go into everything.

But there is no need for that. Exercises are given, for example exercises in self-awareness, or concentration exercises focusing on specific topics. And these also cover what I have just said about the nature of copper. There is no need to write specifically that one must focus on the nature of copper. What is said is that you should take some simple content and concentrate on that each morning and each evening. This is just another way of saying that one can concentrate, for example, on the nature of copper. A possible content for the soul in this context is given, just as one might also refer to the use of metallic substances.

If I say to someone: You should concentrate every morning and every evening on a specific soul content, for example 'wisdom shines in the light', then, if he really does this, it will work in his soul. It would be exactly the same if I were to tell him to learn all about the nature of copper and concentrate on copper. The only difference is that the one is derived from what is moral and the other from what is physical or chemical. And for someone who does not happen to be a chemist it is much better to approach the spiritual world along the path of moral considerations.

These indications might initially sound as though they were intended to qualify the exercises given in *Knowledge of the Higher Worlds* and replace them with more thoughtful soul content rather than that related to the senses.

However, in the extract from the lecture of 15 August 1924 quoted here, what Rudolf Steiner says about living in the senses makes it clear how important he considered pure sense perception to be. This also amplifies the physiological descriptions of pure perception in Chapters 3 and 4. Furthermore, in the many further editions of *Knowledge of the Higher Worlds* he published, Steiner always retained the sense-perception exercises to be used in connection with Preparation and Enlightenment. He did not replace them with other exercises aimed more at thinking, such as those he otherwise gave in relation to the schooling path.

At the end of the lecture on 15 August Steiner also mentioned metals, metallic substances. He had spoken about this in the preceding lecture with regard to ancient humanity. In connection with enhancing a person's awareness, it was evidently the custom in former times to provide pupils of the occult with doses of certain metals in a highly potentized form. With reference to our present time, however, and in connection with anthroposophical medicine Steiner referred to the use of highly potentized metals for curing certain specific diseases.

25. Asafoetida is a stinking gum (known as Devil's Dung) obtained from an umbelliferous plant (*Ferula foetida*).

26. This extract from *Knowledge of the Higher Worlds* (Chapter 5, 'The Conditions of Esoteric Training') directly follows the second passage from that book cited here in Chapter 8. The seven conditions described may be regarded as training for a 'spiritual balance' as indicated with regard to the fourth condition. By working to develop these conditions, an individual striving for supersensible perception becomes able to enter into a breathing, empathetic relationship with the world. Thus the exercises in perception described earlier as being a breathing process of perceiving and thinking are augmented by exercises tending more towards the moral plane. Actually, if

we look more closely we shall notice that none of the exercises, for example those given in Chapter 1 as the exercises of preparation, are ever described purely in isolation, but are always complemented by instructions leading more towards the moral realm.

27. This passage is taken from the essay 'The World-Thoughts in the Working of Michael and in the Working of Ahriman' in *Anthroposophical Leading Thoughts* (CW 26). It is among a series of 'Letters to Members of the Anthroposophical Society' which Rudolf Steiner wrote towards the end of his life when, on account of illness, he was no longer able to give lectures. These letters present anthroposophy in a concentrated form. The Archangel Michael, the Spirit of the Age, appears here as the leading spiritual being with regard to anthroposophy. That Michael is especially linked with the aspect of pure perception is made clear not only in the passage from *The Mission of the Archangel Michael* quoted in Chapter 2 but also here in this excerpt from one of the 'Letters to Members'.

Sources

Rudolf Steiner's works are listed as recorded in the collected works (CW). The works mentioned in the present volume:

CW 4   *The Philosophy of Spiritual Activity*, Rudolf Steiner Press, 1979 (currently published as *The Philosophy of Freedom*).

CW 10   *Knowledge of the Higher Worlds*, Rudolf Steiner Press, 2012. The passages quoted are from the translation by Dorothy Osmond and Charles Davy.

CW 26   *Anthroposophical Leading Thoughts*, Rudolf Steiner Press, 1973.

CW 58   *Transforming the Soul, Vol. 1*, Rudolf Steiner Press, 2005.

CW 66   *The Foundations of Human Experience*, Anthroposophic Press, 1996.

CW 118 *The Reappearance of Christ in the Etheric*, SteinerBooks, 2003.

CW 136 *Spiritual Beings in the Heavenly Bodies and in the Kingdoms of Nature*, Rudolf Steiner Press, 1995.

CW 194 *Michael's Mission*, Rudolf Steiner Press, 2015.

CW 212 *Life of the Human Soul*, Rudolf Steiner Press, 2016.

CW 219 *Man and the World of Stars*, Anthroposophic Press, 1982.

CW 232 *Mystery Knowledge and Mystery Centres*, Rudolf Steiner Press, 1997.

CW 243 *True and False Paths in Spiritual Investigation*, Rudolf Steiner Press, 1969.

CW 268   *Mantric Sayings. Meditations 1903–1925*, SteinerBooks, 2015.

CW 322   *The Boundaries of Natural Science*, Anthroposophic Press, 1983.